REAGAN

MAN OF PRINCIPLE

REAGAN

MAN OF PRINCIPLE

by

John Harmer

COUNCIL·PRESS™

Springville, Utah

ISBN: 1-55517-619-4
v.1

Published by Cedar Fort Inc.
www.cedarfort.com

Distributed by:

Typeset by Kristin Nelson
Cover design by Bryan Twede
Cover design © 2002 by Lyle Mortimer

Cover: photo of Ronald Reagan
Used by permission of station WGBH, Boston, Massachusetts
(Copyright 1973, WGBH/Boston)

Printed in the United States of America
10 9 8 7 6 5 4 3 2 1

Printed on acid-free paper

Library of Congress Cataloging-in-Publication Data

Harmer, John, 1934-
  Reagan : man of principle / by John Harmer ; with Lee Nelson.
    p. cm.
  ISBN 1-55517-619-4 (pbk. : acid-free paper)
  1. Reagan, Ronald--Political and social views. 2. Reagan,
Ronald--Ethics. 3. Social values--United States. 4. Presidents--United
States--Biography. 5. Governors--California--Biography. I. Nelson,
Lee. II. Title.
  E877.2 .H36 2002
  973.927'092--dc21
                              2002004864

DEDICATION

This book about the political life and character of Ronald Reagan is dedicated to the memory of

Sp. 5 ROSS M. BEE,

UNITED STATES ARMY

Ronald Reagan never met or knew anything about Ross Bee, but on every occasion possible he honored him and all who served and sacrificed with him in Vietnam.

On January 18, 1967, while serving in the United StatesArmy in Vietnam, Ross Bee was promoted to Sp.5. Ross was just six months short of his 21st birthday. The next day, January 19, 1967, Ross led his patrol out into the jungle, where in an ambush by the enemy he was shot and killed.

His final resting place is in the family plot in the cemetery in Georgetown, Idaho.

I am confident that it would please Ronald Reagan to know that this little book was dedicated to someone like Ross M. Bee.

TABLE OF CONTENTS

ACKNOWLEDGMENTS

I need to acknowledge the encouragement and contribution of many without whom this little book would never have been possible.

My son David, who with his siblings often heard me recite many of the experiences contained in this book continually urged me to make a record of these very personal and private moments with Governor Ronald Reagan.

I am deeply indebted to Edwin Meese III and to Judge William "Bill" Clark, primarily for their friendship and their example as patriots and men of honor, but also for their willingness to share with me recollections of private moments with Ronald Reagan. In addition to half a dozen lengthy private interviews, Ed Meese, in his capacity as a distinguished visiting fellow at the Hoover Institution on the campus of Stanford University, made it possible for me to have access to the Ronald Reagan gubernatorial papers at the Hoover Archives. Ed also reviewed the initial manuscript and made a number of very helpful recommendations.

After leaving the position of National Security Advisor to the President, Judge Bill Clark remained silent for some sixteen years about the dynamics of what happened inside the Oval Office to bring about the end of the Cold War. I am grateful to him for sharing his insight into the character of Ronald Reagan that constitutes the majority of Chapter Eleven. I'm also deeply grateful to Bill for having remained so loyally attentive to and supportive of Ronald Reagan during the years when Reagan was no longer able to recognize or appreciate that loyalty.

I am particularly indebted to General Amos "Joe" Jordan, (U.S. Army Ret.) for his kindness in reading the entire manuscript and for making a number of valuable editorial suggestions. General Jordan is a remarkable combination of academic excellence and military statesmanship. During his very distinguished career he served his country as a professor at West Point, and as a senior advisor to four different Presidents and their Secretaries of State and Defense.

My dear friend Emerito Estrada-Rivera, of San Juan, Puerto Rico, was equally an admirer of Ronald Reagan. He too never faltered in his urging me to write out these experiences. I remain very much in his debt for that kindness.

I am grateful to Greg Cumming, the curator of the Reagan Presidential Library, for his assistance in obtaining copies of certain documents that were important in the preparation of chapter ten.

I acknowledge the patience of Vladimir Stefanovic, of PBS station WGBH, in Boston, for bearing with me as I continued to insist that somewhere in their archives we could find the videotape of the 1973 Advocates program on which Ronald Reagan and I appeared. My persistence and Vlad's patience finally resulted in finding the tape. It was most helpful in confirming several important conversations with Ronald Reagan recited in the text.

Lee Nelson edited the initial draft of the manuscript and made a number of insightful recommendations which greatly improved the continuity of the text. I am also indebted to Lee for his encouragement to go forward with publishing this text when my own endurance with this project was nearly exhausted.

There are others who deserve much more recognition for having encouraged and facilitated the ability to finally go to press. They include George Biada, a dear friend and business colleague, and Eugene Vezzani, a man whom Ronald Reagan would have enjoyed knowing. Finally, my patient and long suffering wife, Carolyn, mother of our ten children, and the heroic companion of more than forty years, who in victory and defeat never faltered in her love.

INTRODUCTION

I have not written this book to recite what Ronald Reagan did, but to set forth as concisely as possible what he was. I leave to others the burden of defending the Reagan record of accomplishment in Sacramento and Washington D.C. What I have tried to do here is reveal the power for good in Ronald Reagan's life, and underline the character traits which were the ultimate source of his remarkable accomplishments.

This is not a biography of Ronald Reagan. It is simply the story of how one man who worked closely with Reagan for eight years while he was governor of California came to understand the principles that dominated his life. During those eight years I had a number of one-on-one experiences with Ronald Reagan, giving me a glimpse of the inner man, his core values, his attributes and talents. The single most descriptive analysis of Ronald Reagan I can give is that here was a man who had a very clear vision of himself and his objectives. It seemed he could always see through the irrelevant and often noisy distractions to the core issue. I never saw the day when his vision was obscured or unclear. He knew himself, and he had supreme confidence in his ultimate destiny.

Throughout most of my adult life it has been my habit to keep a detailed daily journal. Through the years my journal keeping habits have evolved, but the primary effort has always been to keep an accurate record of my activities and appointments. These journals helped make it possible to reconstruct many of the events described in this book.

Although I had made a number of speeches in support of Ronald Reagan's campaign for president, I did not follow him to Washington. In the fall of 1980 my wife and I had the responsibility to provide for our ten children, the oldest having just begun his university education. We had lived in Washington while I went to law school at the George Washington University. While we loved the city, and the sensation of being near the heart of government, we knew that our first duty was to our children. When the rest of the Reagan team went to Washington we remained in the west.

Many of those who did go to Washington have remained close friends. Among these are Judge William "Bill" Clark and Edwin Meese, III. Ed Meese worked closely with Ronald Reagan throughout his entire sixteen years of public service, as governor and then as president. The references made to the Reagan presidency are primarily taken from conversations with Ed Meese. Judge Bill Clark was my primary source of information in the last chapter.

It was in Sacramento that I saw and studied Ronald Reagan. In retrospect it is obvious that much of his success in the U.S. presidency stems from the tutorial experiences he had as governor of California. For eight years he presided over one tenth of the entire American population. The annual budget for the state of California was the seventh or eighth largest government budget in the entire world. The legislature he dealt with was remarkably similar to the U.S. Congress. The California legislature attracted people of great talent and even greater egos. All of these factors helped prepare Ronald Reagan for the challenges he faced as president.

The justification for writing this book is my conviction that I am providing a very honest and accurate analysis of the character of the man who became the fortieth president of the United States. Ronald Reagan, more than anyone else, changed the course of modern history with the vision and courage by which he ended the Cold War.

During the eight years we worked together in Sacramento, I came to understand many things about Ronald Reagan. One of them was that he never considered politics a "career." For him the political life was a mission, a noble cause, even a religious crusade. I am also certain that in his mind, his calling to that mission came from a divine source.

In the pages that follow I have tried to identify the qualities and principles that comprised the core values of a valiant human being.

ONE

MAN OF PRINCIPLE

It wasn't very many weeks into Ronald Reagan's second term as governor of California in 1970 that people began to realize that "politics as usual" was a term of the past. The actor-cowboy from Los Angeles apparently had no intention of following the play book which prescribed acceptable political behavior as long as anyone could remember. But first, some background.

The California legislature functions more like the U.S. Congress than like most state legislatures. That is partially understandable given the fact that one out of every ten Americans (and probably one out of five of all the illegal aliens) live in California. During the 1970's the California Senate had forty members, but there were nearly fifty members of the U.S. House of Representatives from California. Thus, a state senator had more constituents than a member of the U.S. Congress. The legislative sessions tended to go from January until October, not dissimilar to the national congress. The constant growth of staff to the legislature and the cost of operating the legislature was one of the irresistible consequences of the size and the magnitude of the state.

Article I section 2 of the U.S. Constitution mandates that a census of the citizens be conducted every ten years. That census becomes the basis for the apportionment of representatives in the House of Representatives. It also becomes the basis for the apportionment of representation in state legislatures. Thus, reapportionment, or the establishment of congressional and legislative districts after each census is a constitutionally mandated requirement.

Over the years the political process has evolved a pattern of drawing these lines to favor the party in power. Since the party that holds the majority position in a state legislature controls the reapportionment process, that party does everything possible to create new congressional and legislative district lines to insure the election of its incumbents and to do whatever possible to weaken the position of the minority party.

The individual who first perfected this process was Elbridge Gerry, the governor of Massachusetts, and thus the phrase, "Gerrymandering" came to be associated with the reapportionment process. Gerrymandering is the skillful drawing of new congressional and legislative district lines to enhance the power of the incumbent members and prospective candidates of the majority party.

The process of "reapportionment" often spells life or death for any political incumbent or aspirant who does not deal with a statewide constituency.

As the Republican caucus chairman for the members of the California State Senate, the burden of dealing with the 1970 reapportionment of the state senate fell squarely upon my shoulders. The Republicans held only nineteen of the forty seats in the senate, so we did not dominate the process. However, the Republican governor had the veto power over any bill that he considered unreasonable in the way the various district lines were crafted by the legislature.

The sophistication and overall expense of the process was stunning. Census data was fed into a computer, along with all other available voting record data, so that the political makeup and likely vote of any given neighborhood could be accurately projected. Between the two political parties in the California legislature, the combined expenditure of taxpayer money and funds raised by the respective political parties to support this endeavor came to more than ten million dollars.

However, the purpose of this recital is not to deal with the nuances of the reapportionment process, although they constitute a fascinating story for the political "junkie." In 1971, with the census data and all other available data regarding past voting patterns having been entered into the respective computer data bases, the Republicans and the Democrats in the state legislature continued to joust with one another over the final reapportionment lines. Even the most minute changes in district lines were the subject of continual scrutiny to determine how the change would benefit one party or the other. Members of the U.S. Congress who normally had no contact with the state legislature were constantly on the telephone pleading for assurance that their districts would be protected from any erosion of the essential voter base necessary to keep the incumbents in office.

After months of intense negotiations a compromise bill acceptable to the legislative leadership of both parties was sent to the governor. The assumption was that if the legislative and congressional delegations for whom reapportionment was of the most immediate concern were willing to accept the proposed legislation the governor would accept their recommendation and sign the bill.

This was not a valid assumption when Ronald Reagan was elected governor. He summarily vetoed the bill. I saw months of intense negotiation and thousand of hours of staff work literally evaporate.

After Reagan vetoed the bill I met with him on several occasions to attempt to persuade him that the only way we could resolve the issue was through the contorted process of compromise and negotiation that I had just completed. Reagan was sympathetic with my commitment to the process on behalf of my constituents, and the

Republican members of the senate. However, Reagan was not willing to accept the argument that he should sign a bill that could not be defended solely on the basis of community of interest, grouping the voters together according to common interests and goals. It was one of those occasions when Reagan saw a principle involved, and refused to yield to accommodation, pragmatic political reality, or personal favoritism.

"What exactly do you want?" I asked, in total frustration.

His response was so purely honorable that I dared not repeat it to my senatorial colleagues, knowing they would hoot me out of the room. Yet, though I did not fully appreciate it at the time, the response was just one of many examples of Reagan's strength as a political leader. Reagan, like Thomas Jefferson, had a fundamental faith in the American people and their ability to make the right decisions if they only had all of the facts. Not just the Republicans among the people, but all of the people, once they had all of the facts about any given candidate, would elect the right individuals with the best philosophy of government. On many occasions I marveled at Ronald Reagan's faith in the people, the total body politic. This however, was the most personally painful of those occasions.

What Reagan wanted me to do was very simple.

"Start on the north border of the state," he said, "and come down the state and deal with the legislative and congressional lines in terms of what was best for the people. Ignore party interests. Just look for the community of interest that make sense in terms of having a representative in the legislature or the U.S. Congress, and draw the lines that way. Forget about all of this other data you have gathered. Just go back and do what makes the most sense for the people who will be represented."

He made one other comment that was something of a personal rebuke to me.

"I am really disappointed," he said, "that individual Republicans are so willing to sell out the best interests of the people in order to save themselves. That is not what I regard as worthy of my signature."

I left his office wondering how I would ever deal with the irresistible force of a legislature seeking self-preservation and the immovable object, a governor for whom principle was more important than political expediency.

As Reagan and I continued to meet on the issue the problem of the upcoming election cycle in 1972 became more and more of a factor in creating pressure to resolve the issue. On Thursday and Friday, October 28 and 29, 1971, I had five separate meetings with Reagan attempting to find sufficient common ground so he would sign the bill. However, it was impossible for me to reconcile for Reagan the basic political motivation surrounding the specifics of the reapportionment process and his own determination that he would settle for nothing that could not be defended as being best for the people.

In our last meeting on the issue he summed it up in his own matchless capacity to see to the heart of an issue and the fundamental principle involved.

"John," he said, "I'm as dedicated to the Republican cause as you are. Our party's core philosophy represents the best assurance for the continued freedom and prosperity of the nation. But I am not the governor of just the Republicans. There are millions of people out there who, whether they voted for me or not, expect me to represent them with good judgement and integrity. The issue is not one of protecting what you call *the Republican base*. The issue is to do that which is right in principle. The legislators cannot divorce themselves from their own political interests, so I'm going to do it for them. We'll just take the matter away from the legislature and let the court appoint a master who will draw the lines along valid *communities of interest.*

Then he just sat looking at me for a moment, and concluded with a soft-spoken but clearly resolute firmness in his voice, "This is my decision."

With Reagan's final veto of the bill the matter did go to a court appointed master, who did draw the lines. There is justification for some debate as to whether those lines were any more suited to *community of interest* than those we had proposed. But that is not the issue here. In the midst of intense pressure from members of his own party, whose support and assistance were essential to his success, Ronald Reagan looked though the chaff to the wheat, to the core principle involved, and on that core principle he stood firm and made his decision.

I didn't like it. In my situation it was a singular defeat. But in retrospect I genuinely honor him for the integrity of his motive demonstrated in this and a thousand other situations, so much so that I am compelled to write this book so I can share my observations with others.

I am perplexed by the continual reference to Reagan as an *enigma*, or *man of mystery*. Ronald Reagan was one of the most open and transparent individuals I have ever known. It would be difficult to imagine anyone who was more predictable or more consistent. Reagan was in private exactly as he was in public. There was no" Jekyl and Hyde" duality in Ronald Reagan.

I am also convinced that many of those who were around him in Sacramento, and who had every opportunity to measure the man and his basic character, never really seemed to grasp who and what he was. They kept looking beyond the mark. For some reason they could never accept the fact that someone of that charisma could be exactly what he appeared to be. They were always suspicious that he was still the actor, that he never let them see the real man.

I first met Ronald Reagan in 1962. I was the campaign manager for a Republican candidate for congress in the western portion of the San Fernando Valley in Los Angeles County. The candidate was Steve Foote. He had a lot of heart but there was precious little money in the campaign bank account.

Ronald Reagan had been giving some patriotic talks in the southern California area. As we struggled to find a mechanism to raise money for the Foote campaign, one of our campaign workers suggested contacting Reagan and asking if he would be the featured speaker at a fund raising dinner for our candidate. Reagan graciously agreed to come. The night of that dinner in 1962 was when I met Ronald Reagan.

We chatted amiably prior to his speech, and talked about current events, the Nixon campaign for governor, and political philosophy. During the meal he took out his 3 x 5 cards to make some last minute adjustments to his talk. Then finally the time came for him to take the podium. The talk was classic Reagan, even then. He ranged over the entire spectrum of conservative issues. With devastating effectiveness, he kept the audience on the edge of their seats for nearly forty-five minutes. At the end he received an extended standing ovation. The talk and evening so energized the campaign team that we remained at the headquarters until nearly three in the morning recounting the wonder of the evening and Reagan's incredible speech in behalf of our candidate.

In writing a thank-you letter to Reagan I was presumptuous enough to urge him to consider the race for the U.S. Senate in 1964. I outlined all of the reasons why I was confident he could obtain the Republican nomination and go on to win the senate seat. I concluded the letter with this observation:

The Republican message is still searching for a great messenger—this state still needs a great spokesman in Washington.

You could become both, at a time when you are needed most.

Reagan responded with a letter dated December 12, 1962, in which he said:

> *Thanks very much for your kind letter and offer of help. At the moment, however, I think I'll continue speaking for other people. I have never seriously considered politics as a career.*

During the next few months we exchanged several more letters. I did not see him again until the campaign of 1964. Reagan helped his old friend George Murphy win election to the United States Senate from California. But the real story of 1964 was the Reagan speech on national television on behalf of Senator Barry Goldwater, the Republican candidate for president. The first time I heard Ronald Reagan give that speech was during a campaign rally for Goldwater out in the San Fernando Valley. All of the Republican candidates for congress and state legislative offices were invited, and the featured speaker was Ronald Reagan.

Most people remember 1964 because of the talk on national television, but it was in Los Angeles, where Reagan first electrified the audience, that Reagan was introduced to the world of presidential politics. I am convinced that it was on that night that he first envisioned the possibility that he could and would become president of the United States.

The next time we met was in September, 1966. Reagan was now the Republican nominee for governor of California, and I was the Republican candidate for the California State Senate in the twenty-first senatorial district. Reagan made a campaign appearance in the heart of my district, the city of Glendale. I was seated next to him. He remembered our prior meetings and conversations. He joked about the fact that I had tried to get him to run for the U.S. Senate, and now I was a candidate seeking election to the state senate.

Ten years later, in 1976, Reagan was seeking the Republican nomination for U.S. president. His opponent was the incumbent, President Gerald Ford. The Republican national convention was held in Kansas City. As a former Lt. Governor to Reagan I was asked to speak to several of the state delegations regarding his record as governor of California. During one of these talks Reagan and several campaign aids appeared in the back of the room. He listened as I completed my recital of his accomplishments and proven ability as governor, and then he came forward to speak to the delegates. As we shook hands, he said, "Thanks for the kind words, I'm grateful for your help." I reminded him that he had once told me that he had never seriously considered politics as a career.

Throughout those eight years when he served as governor I gradually became aware of several essential factors about the man and his basic nature. I came to understand how he fashioned his political philosophy. He had been making hundreds of speeches for the General Electric Company. All across the United States he had been before audiences of average Americans. In his research for these talks Reagan studied the works of the founding fathers, the writings of the great political philosophers, the commentaries of the political journalists of our day. In the process he forged a core philosophy of freedom and constitutional government that became his frame of reference for all that he did in public office.

Let me illustrate just one example. In a speech on an October evening in 1962 he made a reference to the Cold War, in which he said:

> ...we're not war mongers, we're not trying to send other people's sons to war; we have sons of our own. We believe in peace, but we know that appeasement does not give a choice between peace and

war, only between fight or surrender.

Eighteen years before he was elected President, Ronald Reagan had clearly defined in his own mind that the Cold War had to end in victory over communism, not in appeasement. Throughout his time of preparation for the office of president he remained true to that principle, and the many others that were forged into his character through his own research of history and the writings of the founding fathers.

One other vital element of all those speeches was what I like to call the *spiritual* chemistry that developed between Ronald Reagan and his audiences. Through their questions and comments he learned to understand what the American people felt and thought and wanted from their government. Throughout his political career he would often find new strength and renewed conviction by going back to the American people.

He could work all day in Sacramento, and when others about him were exhausted he would be eager to fly to Los Angeles for another one of the hundreds of speaking engagements to which he was committed. When I was with him I could sense the bonding of kindred spirits between Reagan and his audience. From these experiences he seemed to glean renewed zeal for his grand crusade.

Reagan's conversion to the conservative philosophy of limiting the political and economic power of government was both intellectual and visceral. As he appeared before audiences made up of middle class America, many of them blue collar workers, he could sense that they too yearned for less government and less restraint by government upon their economic dreams. These were the people whom he came to trust, who sensed instinctively the danger of a government out of control. His message and his dream of a greater America, because it was a freer America, never faltered. And invariably, when he needed help to push forward some essential part of his program, it was to the American people that he would turn for help.

At the same time, I came to admire his leadership skills, particularly his ability to negotiate with political opponents who presumably held the majority of power. Reagan was a master negotiator. He had an ability to sense what he could accomplish, and even though his advisors were often doubtful that he could attain his goal, he would persevere and almost always succeed. It is true that he seldom obtained everything he wanted, but it is equally true that he never lost hope in ultimately accomplishing what that core sense of values told him was best for the people. And if all else failed, he would go to the people to strengthen his case against those who opposed him. It was stunning to see him motivate an audience to pick up the banner that he held out for them and march forward in the cause which he asked them to serve.

I never heard Ronald Reagan enunciate a set of *rules* or *core values* that guided his life. Yet, on many occasions, he would make a comment regarding a government program or individual that would reveal a fundamental principle which governed Reagan's personal and political life.

Ronald Reagan lived and acted in harmony with principles. This is the reason he could carry on in the face of significant opposition or momentary defeat. He knew that the principle was right, and ultimately his adherence to the principle would bring him the victory.

I came to recognize that much of Reagan's strength lay in his honesty with himself and others. If a question arose, either in a press conference or in his private office, to which he did not know or have an answer, he never tried to bluff his way through it. In a number of private and public situations I saw him turn to one of his aides for an explanation of the question, sometimes getting the answer, sometimes not. Once he understood the question he gave an answer that reflected the political and philosophical standard involved, even if he did not have the specific details in mind. He could be comfortable doing that because his approach to any problem was based on his commitment to principle. Once the issue at hand was clear it seemed relatively easy for him to apply the principle or principles that in his mind governed that issue.

Ed Meese put it this way:

He was not a "preachy" type. He believed deeply in his principles—but you had to see them in action to get them defined. He did not set out a list of things that he believed and felt he had to pursue.

Principle motivated everything he did. Example: Freedom fighters in Nicaragua. He had tremendous opposition to the idea of supporting them—but he would not allow that opposition to let him forget the principle involved. Tip O'Neil, the Speaker of the House of Representatives, was a ferocious opponent of Reagan's determination to support the Nicaragua Freedom fighters. So was his successor, Jim Wright. But Reagan knew that the principle was correct, and he never wavered from his commitment to the principle of supporting people's struggle for freedom anywhere in the world.

Another area along the same lines was his firm belief that the 'doctrine of mutual assured destruction was immoral. He also felt it was militarily and diplomatically impractical. He worried that at some time a Soviet leader would miscalculate that the Americans would not launch a response and that miscalculation could lead us into a war. He thought that the failure to have a defense against a nuclear missile was a grievous exposure of the nation to destruction. So that is why he went to Cheyenne Mountain in 1979 to visit the NORAD. Why he insisted that the Chiefs of Staff commit themselves to dealing with this issue. He was ridiculed for his "Star Wars" doctrine, but he was determined to see it become a reality because there were fundamental principles upon which his commitment was based.

The principles comprising the core convictions in Ronald Reagan's life became apparent in the priorities he set forth as governor. He consistently sought for ways to reduce the imposition of government into the lives of citizens because he fervently believed in the principle that excessive government destroys freedom. Yet, Reagan was not a libertarian. He knew that there were some things that the national government was best suited to accomplish, such as defense. His experience as governor made him conscious of the tenth amendment, and he seriously pursued reducing the federal government's intrusion into matters he knew the writers of the constitution felt were best left to the states.

To him maximum freedom was an essential element of a truly great nation. He was convinced that those who contributed most to the happiness, prosperity, and fundamental welfare of all the people were those whose creativity and productivity in commerce brought abundance to the entire social spectrum. Reagan did not want government officials to stifle the creativity of the entrepreneur. He was firmly committed to the proposition that the best social welfare program was one that did the most to enhance the creative forces in the individual and the world of commerce.

This did not mean that he was blind to reality, to the excesses that unprincipled economic exploitation could bring about. Reagan believed in justice, and was furious when businesses took unfair advantage of employees or consumers. On many occasions he personally intervened when he became aware of conduct that he believed to be unjust or inequitable.

On one occasion, during a meeting with legislative leaders, someone mentioned a news story about a scheme that had cost hundreds of senior citizens their life's savings. The plight of the victims was discussed with little sympathy for the victims. After listening to the discussion Reagan erupted with uncharacteristic bitterness. He was furious that someone would be so far beyond decency and sensitivity for others to be able to perpetrate such an injustice. Most everyone in the room was startled at the vehemence of his reaction.

Ronald Reagan seemed constantly aware of the plight of the elderly and the financially downtrodden. That awareness did not mean that anything and everything the state government wanted to do in the name of welfare services was prudent or useful. He constantly struggled to *cut, squeeze, and trim* the cost of government, because he strongly believed that government has an insatiable appetite for power over the lives of the governed, which includes the power to tax away the people's wealth. That principle did not preclude striving to help the needy but he fought those who wanted to transfer wealth from the rich to the poor to attract more votes.

Through Reagan's personal research into the writings of the founding fathers and the great political philosophers, justice for the individual became part of his intellectual and philosophical framework. By the end of his second year as governor, because of his experiences in dealing with bureaucracies and liberal legislators, the principle of needing to reduce intrusion by government had become a driving conviction.

I have a transcript of the first political speech Ronald Reagan gave in 1962. In it he presents the principles that would become and remain the driving thrust of his political philosophy. Though he may not have accomplished all he wanted as governor and president, what he did accomplish came about because of these principles. Though the pathway he followed as the chief executive of California, and then the nation, had to zig-zag in order to continue going forward, his vision of what would provide maximum freedom and prosperity to the American people never wavered or deviated.

In that first speech he used one phrase and asked one question that he often repeated, usually in front of an audience, but sometimes just in the privacy of his office. These two quotes from that speech are the essence of Ronald Reagan's character and his legacy as one of history's most remarkable leaders. They were:

> *You and I have a rendezvous with destiny.*
> *And,*
> *Will we pledge our lives and our sacred honor?*

From that speech, given in the fall of 1962, which resounded so powerfully in the hearts of that California audience, one can find the beacons of light that were to guide him through the next thirty years. He began with an observation that was important to him then and remained important to him throughout his public life.

"I have just a few notes here of my own. My ideas, my words, are my own," he said.

Long before he had the luxury of speech writers, Ronald Reagan gave hundreds of speeches filled with his own ideas in his own words. The speech writers of later years provided new framework, but the essential tapestry was his own and it never changed.

Reagan went on to say:

> *The Republican Party is polarized around a belief in govern-*
> *ment rooted in the local community, rather than in some far distant*
> *capitol, with power limited to the least amount necessary for the*
> *performance of its duties, a belief that free men can provide for*
> *themselves better than government can do this for them. By their*
> *own words, the leadership of the Democratic Party is committed to*
> *a belief that our traditional system of individual liberty and local*

rule are no longer capable of meeting the complex problems of the Twentieth Century. They've placed a faith in government playing a more important role, including a government-directed and planned economy."

Such a change in our traditional system of individual freedom is advanced as an answer to the Cold War. According to one government advisor, we can have peace without victory, peace without conflict, by 'a peaceful transition into a not undemocratic socialism.'"

"In other words, as we move to the left into a planned economy, the enemy will give up his fear and mistrust and he will move to the right and meet us, or, as the poet Frost said upon his return from Moscow, 'the Communists are coming down to Socialism,' I challenge his choice of directions when he said, 'we are coming up from Capitalism to Socialism.'"

"Thus the Lion and the Lamb will lie down together, which is a great philosophy if we can afford to throw in a fresh lamb every morning..."

"Our friends seek the answer to all the problems of human need through government. Freedom can be lost inadvertently in this way. Government tends to grow; it takes on a weight and momentum in government programs that goes far beyond the original purpose that caused their creation. This is what Thomas Jefferson had in mind when he predicted future happiness for the people if we can prevent government from wasting the labors of the people under the pretense of taking care of them..."

"A government may be the most benevolent, the most well-meaning in the world, but when it attempts to control the economy and operate the production of a nation, it must eventually use coercion and force to achieve it purposes.

"...When we question proposed social reforms, usually we are challenged that we lack humanity. No responsible person would

suggest that our senior citizens, for example, who reach their non-earning years without savings or pensions should be denied a livelihood. And yet, most responsible citizens, all of us as a matter of fact, should ask some questions about the present social security program..."

"...If money is an answer to our educational problems, has the government found some new source other than our pockets? And, if the government increases the amount it takes from those pockets, is it not decreasing the amount left for local taxation, for contributions to private educational and charitable institutions?

...I think that Christian charity—charity of the God of Moses, requires that we should share of our surplus goods with our needy neighbors, but I don't think it requires us to go into debt to see that he has an egg in his beer.

...No nation in history has ever survived a tax burden that reached a third of its national income... We need tax reform of what the personal income tax, the graduated tax, has done to the great American dream...

...But we'd better make sure we have representatives in Washington who will determine the tax reform will be accompanied by an end to deficit spending, that our government will be forced to stay within the limits of its revenue...we must see that tax reform reduces the percentage of income taken by the federal government...We can give our children a heritage of freedom because freedom is never more than one generation away from extinction, or we can leave them with a debt that can only be paid by inflating the value out of their earnings. We can restore the constitutional limits on government power.

Daniel Webster said, "Hold on, my friends, to the Constitution of the United States of America and to the Republic for which it stands. Miracles do not cluster. What has happened once in six thou-

sand years may never happen again. Hold on to your Constitution for if the Constitution shall fall, there will be anarchy throughout the world." It has been said that if we lose this way of ours, this traditional freedom, history will report with the greatest astonishment that those who had the most to lose, did the least to prevent it happening.

...You and I have a rendezvous with destiny; we'll meet the challenge in the days ahead or we'll trail in the dust the golden hope of mankind for years to come. Are we a different breed of American? Has life become so dear and peace so sweet as to be purchased at the price of chains of slavery? Or, will we pledge our lives and our sacred honor?

...We're not war mongers, we're not trying to send other people's sons to war; we have sons of our own. We believe in peace, but we know that appeasement does not give a choice between peace and war, only between fight or surrender.

In a speech given eighteen years before he became president, Ronald Reagan verbalized the principles he thought should be the guiding philosophy of the U.S. President in dealing with the Cold War. Appeasement does not give a choice between peace and war, only between fight or surrender. As president his strategy was to win a victory in the Cold War, not to continue the politics of appeasement.

In his personal life there were qualities and principles of behavior that were never referred to by name but were often revealed by his conduct and his conversation. One had only to see Reagan's demeanor and hear the way he analyzed an issue to be able to identify those qualities and principles. Ronald Reagan always extended to those who opposed him or ridiculed him far more deference, respect, and consideration for their opinions than they extended to him.

When Reagan would read in a daily newspaper or national slick magazine a demeaning characterization of himself he would usually laugh, or make some insightful comment to illustrate why something he had said or done could justify the negative assertion. Some of his favorite political cartoons were from the liberal press in Sacramento and San Francisco. Reagan was always capable of laughing at himself and appreciating the ability of an editorial cartoonist to capture some issue in a humorous way. He never wasted his time or emotional reserve by denigrating someone who differed with him. He never allowed his critics to entice him down to their level of conduct.

I have never heard anyone refer to Ronald Reagan as a humble man. Yet, on many occasions, I saw him demonstrate a very literal degree of both humility and kindness. I was his junior by twenty-five years, yet he never exhibited anything but respect and honest consideration for my views. Even on several occasions when the exchange between us became heated and intense as we disagreed on some current issue of policy or legislative enactment, his demeanor and his language was tempered out of respect for the opinions of others and a quality of humility in himself that reminded him that he too was only mortal.

For Reagan the compliments, the adulation, and the hero worship, were no different than their opposites, the denigration and the demeaning characterizations. In his own mind both were equally unwarranted. As a man of principle he had no difficulty being faithful to the course upon which he had set his sights. Expediency of conduct, either to court favor or to deflect criticism were never acceptable forms of behavior He never made reference to some political victory or accomplishment in a personal sense. He would graciously give recognition or credit to others, but never sought if for himself.

Given the adulation and hero worship that often characterized those who came to the governor's office to meet Ronald Reagan, or the superlatives that were used to introduce him at events in which he was the featured attraction, it is incredible that he remained as personally gracious and unaffected by it all as he did. When we were at political gatherings he would be the recipient of both private and public expressions of adoration that could have made him arrogant beyond description. He seemed to let these roll off his back with the same equanimity that he exhibited toward the continued efforts of the media and his political opponents to paint him as an "acting" Governor.

On one occasion I told him a true story from my own family situation. My wife and I always tried to end the day by having our children gather with us for family prayer. On one occasion after a particularly long and intense day in the capitol I came home late to find the children asleep. Before retiring my wife and I had the usual prayer. When it was over she said to me, " I think you need a rest. You have been be working too hard."

"Why do you say that?" I asked.

"Because," she responded, "three times during our prayer you referred to the Lord as 'Governor.'"

When I told Reagan that story he laughed and said, "Well, that helps balance out the people who are constantly referring to me as the other guy from the pit of fire and brimstone."

If I ever saw Reagan depict something other than genuine respect for another person, it was on those several occasions when he was asked to receive an individual of intellectual prominence; not only from the United States, but from other parts of the world as well. As governor of California he was often asked to give an audience to someone who brought with them an international reputation for intellectuality. Since portions of my State Senate district represented some of the most prestigious areas of Los Angeles County, I sometimes had a constituent ask me to facilitate a meeting with the governor on behalf of a distinguished visitor.

On several occasions I was witness to situations where a visitor came filled with too much belief in his own publicity. If Reagan sensed from his visitor any degree of arrogance or pomposity it seemed to me that he would engage in a banter or the recitation of one of the hundreds of humorous stories at his command. He would intentionally give the impression that he either had no interest in the profound thoughts with which his visitor wanted to impress the governor or had no ability to relate them to anything with which he was concerned. At first perplexed by this behavior, I came to the conclusion that it was an expression of Reagan's dislike of vanity and his difficulty in making conversation with people who had solutions to all the world's problems, but as Reagan once said to me, "…couldn't figure how to put on a pair of matching stockings in the morning."

I also accompanied on visits to the governor's office academics, legislative leaders from other states, and respected leaders of national organizations who were concerned with great social issues. He was always equal to the challenge of reasoning with these individuals. On one occasion I met with Reagan and Nobel Economist Milton Freedman. For over an hour the discussion ranged over the entire spectrum of national and international economic issues. Reagan was totally capable of engaging in a very detailed analysis of these issues.

During the three years that I was chairman of the Republican Caucus in the State Senate I sometimes accompanied legislative leaders from other states to their appointments with Reagan. Though they came to ask how he accomplished some of the outstanding achievements of his administration, he was ever willing to give credit to others. Reagan never said, "I did this or I did that…" He always said "we…"

In these meetings his decorum was ever gracious. He received his visitors warmly but did not attempt any undue familiarity. Reagan could discuss in specific detail almost any issue that they raised. He could give encouragement and insight without becoming condescending. It was his knowledge of the specifics about social, educational, and political issues that made it clear that there was depth and substance in his leadership.

Ed Meese told me of a comment that Reagan had made after returning to the Capitol from one of the retreats of the Bohemian Club of California, probably the most exclusive gathering of influential and powerful individuals within the state. To become one of the Bohemian Club regulars is a status that many of the lesser lights in the world of industry, commerce, science and politics in California covet but rarely achieve.

After returning from one of the annual Bohemian Club retreats at the "grove" where he was, as usual, the center of tremendous interest even among individuals of great national and international prominence, Ed Meese asked the Governor how he enjoyed himself. Reagan's response was classic Ronald Reagan:

"You know, Ed," he said, "a little of that goes a long way."

TWO

HONOR & INTEGRITY

"My honor is my life; both grow in one; Take honor from me, and my life is done."
—Shakespeare: King Richard II: Act 1, sc. 1, line 182

As World War II was unleashed upon the United States and the intensive effort to recruit men into military service increased, Ronald Reagan knew that because of his poor eyesight he would probably be classified 4-F, meaning he could avoid military service altogether. Reagan chose instead to join the reserves as an enlisted man. He worked his way up to an officer's status. Because of his eyesight he could never go into combat, but he believed very strongly that everyone had a duty to make whatever sacrifice they could for the national cause.

Reagan was assigned to work with the Army Air Corps in the development of training films. Several of the films that he helped script and then narrated became training classics, and were used to train pilots for combat throughout the war.

When the war was over and Reagan was to return to civilian life he declined a promotion from captain to major just prior to his discharge from active duty. Whatever the benefits of accepting the promotion might have been, Reagan's attitude was that he had joined the military to serve, not to exploit, and he asked only that he be able to return to his former life. Service and honor were fundamental values of his essential character. Whenever I saw him in the company of men and women who were serving in the nation's military it was evident that he had an especially high regard for them and for those principles of service and honor that their uniforms represented.

But it was difficult to determine exactly where those values came from. Every once in awhile he would demonstrate his familiarity with history and philosophy by referring to some historical event or individual. He did not just quote things that others had said about these individuals, he had done the reading himself. On one occasion I shared with him a favorite quotation from Michael Montaigne. He responded with a brief discussion about Montaigne's childhood, and how his father had made certain that Montaigne awoke every morning to the sound of classical music from a string quartet.

In various cabinet meetings in Sacramento Reagan would illustrate the point in question by making reference to someone else whose government had faced the same problem. These references could be to someone as remote as Diocletion or as recent as Winston Churchill.

Reagan had a way of testing an idea or a proposed course of action. I never heard him verbalize the test, but I saw him apply it often enough that I could recognize when he was attempting to measure the propriety of what was under consideration. In a word the test was whether or not the proposed action or decision was *honorable*. I could tell he was finished with his test when he said, "I could defend that in front of an audience as being honorable."

His method of determining whether or not something was honorable was to visualize himself defending it before or with someone whose values he respected.

Besides his wife, Nancy, and his brother Neil, Ronald Reagan had great faith in one other fountain of wisdom and truth—the people he represented. From three sources he sought confirmation of what was right. From the same three sources he found strength and renewal. Reagan could spend an entire day working with legislative leaders and members of his administration and then fly to somewhere in California to participate in the never ending process of fund raising and sustaining the local political organization. Even after a grueling day of negotiations, Reagan would find in these *rubber chicken* dinners a rapport with the people that would ignite in him the confirmation of what path he should follow, and help him renew his strength and stamina to go at it again the next day.

Richard Nixon, who I believe was prepared to execute the office of president as effectively as any man who ever sought to become president, was ultimately destroyed by the American media. Ronald Reagan, equally despised by the overwhelmingly liberal working press, was never beaten by the liberal media. He simply would use his masterful powers of communication to go beyond their misrepresentation of his purpose and conviction and rally the support of the American people. It was in the response from the people, the unity and harmony of his conviction with theirs, that Reagan found his most sustaining source of strength.

Although I had several meetings with him, I certainly never knew Richard Nixon as I did Ronald Reagan. I have the impression that an essential part of Nixon's style of leadership was manipulation of individuals. Those who knew Nixon closely may reject that assessment as unfair, or without any valid foundation. Whether that is accurate or not, I can say categorically that Reagan was never manipulative of other people. He didn't have to be. His own charisma, his clear-cut commitment to principles and his ability to verbalize his objectives generally gave others an instant desire to share his vision. The exceptions were political competitors like Tip O'Neil and Ted Kennedy, who seemed determined to oppose him at all costs.

In confrontations with political opponents, it was that vision and certainty of purpose that made Reagan the master of the situation.

These same qualities enabled him to prevail whenever the arrogant and cynical media thought they could knock "this cowboy movie actor out of the saddle."

Reagan had an almost religious reverence for the work and the writings of the founding fathers. That reverence created within him the patriotism that was a fundamental part of his character and his frame of reference. I was with him on several occasions when something was said or done that could not have been anticipated and for which there could not have been a pre-determined reaction. In those instances, whether prompted by a statement or someone's conduct, there would be an instinctive response from Reagan that would reveal his very deep sense of loyalty to the work and the writing of the founding fathers. Sometimes he would simply say, "Madison would be surprised to know that the constitution permitted that..." Sometimes the reaction would be only a gesture, a military salute, or an affirmative nod of the head. Whether by spoken word or body language, Reagan's intense feeling of patriotism and reverence for the legacy of such things as the *Federalist Papers* and the sacrifices of the founding fathers, or the forgotten veterans of past military conflicts, was very real.

I saw him on several occasions meet with veterans who had returned from the conflict in Vietnam. In his demeanor during such visits and his comments afterward one could discern his great respect for them. If they came home disabled he was especially anxious to honor them for their sacrifice. The only time I heard Ronald Reagan swear was in reference to those who left the United States to avoid military obligation.

Reagan would often turn to the Declaration of Independence to borrow a phrase that he wanted to use in a talk. The phrase that usually brought the most emotion to his voice was from the concluding paragraph of the Declaration: "...we mutually pledge to each other our lives, our fortunes, and our sacred honor." For Reagan his "sacred honor" was the sum total of the truth in his life. For Nancy, for his brother Neil, for the people who believed in him, his guiding beacon was his honor. It was the fabric that held everything together when others tried to persuade him that compromise from principle was justified. His honor kept him on an undeviating course.

When President Nixon decided to initiate the restoration of diplomatic relations with China, he realized that one of the most difficult areas of concern was the relationship between the United States and Taiwan. He also realized that of all the potential domestic opponents for his strategy, no one was more capable of mobilizing nationwide rejection of the Nixon strategy than Ronald Reagan. So Nixon sent Henry Kissinger to California to personally brief Reagan on the implications of the strategy. Nixon also decided to ask Reagan to go to Taiwan and personally present Nixon's rationale for the new strategy to the leader of the nationalist Chinese in Taiwan, Chaing Kai Shek.

Reagan was a great admirer of Chaing Kai Shek and believed in the Republic of China. But Reagan's sense of honor and integrity filled him with concern about making any mis-representation to Chaing. At the same time, since the president of the United States had personally appealed to him to make the journey it was impossible to say no.

In preparation for the trip Reagan went to great length to famil-iarize himself with the current situation and the potential for conflict in the Formosa Straits. That intensity of preparation was very useful for Reagan when he became president, and would need to give a clear signal to the communist Chinese leadership about his attitude and intentions regarding the protection of Taiwan from communist aggression.

The Governor took Nancy and their son, Ronnie, with him to

Taiwan. The meetings may have been his baptism by fire in the world of international relations. His greatest concern was that he not fail the president of the United States, but at the same time be honorable with Chang Kai Shek. When Reagan returned he was relieved that he had been able to deal with Chiang in a forthright and honorable manner.

Ronald Reagan struggled to make certain he would never have to explain or apologize for something he had said or done that in retrospect was not totally honorable and forthright. He did not deal with individuals or governments in a duplicitous or devious manner. He also made it clear to those associated with him that not only was that his own standard of official and personal conduct, but he expected it to be theirs as well.

Though staff and official appointees were not always faithful to his wishes in this regard, he made it clear to them that he did not want "political considerations" to influence decisions concerning government policy. Reagan personally was true to this standard of integrity, best illustrated in his judicial appointments. Individuals chosen for appointment to the bench were selected on the basis of merit, and merit alone was the deciding factor. I personally appealed to the governor for the appointment to the bench of a long time friend of his who had also been an activist in the Republican Party. Reagan and the man had known each other on a first name basis for many years. The individual involved was a reasonably competent attorney.

However, there were a number of potential appointees whose intellectual and professional stature exceeded those of Reagan's long time friend. Though the man appealed to me for over a year to remind the Governor of his old friend's long standing application for appointment to the bench, and I did in fact remind the Governor on a number of occasions, the appointment never came.

Notwithstanding the old friendship, Reagan's sense of integrity made it impossible for him to compromise his personal sense of honor which mandated him to provide the people of California with the finest possible judicial appointees.

Reagan expressed his feelings concerning the judiciary at the time he announced the appointment of Chief Justice Rhenquist. It was typical Reagan. He noted his great reverence for the U.S. Constitution and for the work of the founding fathers. What we want "…is not a liberal or a conservative supreme court but one that applies the law and the constitution as written." He was much opposed to an activist judiciary, people who used the judicial bench to further socially popular legislation with no constitutional merit.

Another example of Reagan's integrity was his deference to his successor, George Bush. The Bush tax increase of 1990 was a repudiation of what Reagan considered to be one of his most important legacies as president, the restoration of the nation's economic prosperity through tax cuts. Yet, according to Ed Meese, after leaving the White House Reagan never uttered a critical word about the Bush presidency. Meese said,

"He never really spoke much about it—he did not want to be critical of Bush. He was very pleased with the results of the Gulf War—he felt that he had taken a part in making that happen. Insofar as the rest of the Bush presidency was concerned, Reagan simply felt that it was not appropriate for him to comment on how Bush conducted himself as president. He felt that Bush deserved not to be second guessed by a man no longer holding office."

A lesser man might have found opportunity to express his displeasure at the way in which President Bush and his administration seemed to have forgotten the lessons of the Reagan years.

Ed Messe describes how Reagan instructed Meese, as the attorney general, to deal with the disclosure that Colonel Oliver

North had authorized the unlawful diversion of funds to the Nicaraguan freedom fighters. Meese described his conversation with President Reagan as follows:

"It was Monday morning. Over that weekend I had learned the essential facts of the Iran-Contra matter. The legitimate Iran initiative had been compromised by diversion of funds from the Iran effort to the Contra matter. At 11:15 I met with the president and informed him of what I had learned so far and what I was confident the further disclosures would reveal.

" Reagan said to me, '…whatever the facts may be, let's get to the bottom of it and get the facts out in the open. There is to be no coverup. Whatever is to be done will be done in the full light of all the facts openly disclosed to the congress and the nation.'"

Meese points out that Reagan took immediate steps to deal with the situation. He informed the cabinet, the congress, and the media. He immediately dismissed those responsible, even though that hurt him personally. This cost him the services of his national security advisor, a man who had spent his entire life in service to his country. It also meant losing Col. Oliver North, whose many worthy accomplishments were totally forgotten in the aftermath of Iran-Contra. Reagan genuinely liked Oliver North, and genuinely regretted having to see him go—but he was not willing to compromise the integrity of his administration.

Finally, Reagan had to admit his own error and apologized to the nation. The decision to be totally honest and fully disclose all the details probably saved his presidency. Reagan would not have survived the Iran-Contra matter had he not been so determined to be honest and candid with the nation and the congress.

THREE

THE LEADER

In watching Reagan deal with the legislative leaders of the Democratic Party, I came to admire his capacity as both leader and strategist. For several years prior to the 1966 election, the undisputed boss of the California legislature was assemblyman Jess Unruh. Through the skillful use of his position as speaker of the assembly, Unruh had gained control over the destiny of any piece of legislation, and he used that control to extort massive financial contributions for the political campaign funds he controlled. He would dole out these funds to hapless candidates who would pledge to him their absolute fealty, including letting Unruh tell them how to vote.

The conventional wisdom around Sacramento after the November 1966 election was that *Ronald Reagan may be governor, but Jess Unruh will tell Reagan what to do and when.* It was widely assumed that Reagan—never having held political office before, never having been bruised, battered and scared in the political infighting associated with legislative enactments—would be *dead meat* in the hands of *Big Daddy* Unruh. It never happened.

As the month of January, 1967 opened the new legislative year, the media gleefully anticipated Jess Unruh's first series of lessons for the newly elected governor. Brilliant, ruthless, and exceptionally vulgar, Unruh was anxiously preparing to intimidate the new governor with a display of his raw power.

Ronald Reagan was neither impressed nor intimidated. He carefully took the measure of *Big Daddy*, the nickname the media had picked for Unruh, and went forward with clarity of vision and singularity of purpose. No one, particularly the cynical Unruh, thought that Reagan seriously believed the things he had promised the voters in his first campaign for governor.

From their first encounter in the governor's office Unruh quickly came to realize that this movie actor had a depth and an inner strength that totally belied the back room newspaper propaganda about Reagan that Unruh had come to believe. Jack Lindsey, the governor's legislative liaison to the state assembly, sat in the meeting and shared this description of what happened with me.

"In the midst of telling Governor Reagan what the legislative priorities would be for the coming year, Unruh noticed that the man behind the desk was not only smiling slightly and looking at him, but into him, and straight through him. When the speaker was finished, the Governor simply said, 'I appreciate your briefing. We have our own legislative agenda and at the appropriate time will be happy to share it with you.' That brief statement from Reagan was the end of meeting."

Within a few months the tables had completely turned. Unruh still had the superiority of the majority in both houses of the legislature, but Ronald Reagan was clearly the master of the capital. The people of California began to hear from the governor's office about the specific proposals promised during the campaign that Reagan was now preparing to implement. And the men and women in the assembly who had given their unequivocal commitment to Unruh began hearing from the ultimate source of power, the people whom they represented. And overwhelmingly, the voters were making it clear that they wanted Ronald Reagan to be given the support he needed to carry out his programs. Unruh once said to Jack Lindsey, that Ronald Reagan was the most underrated individual he had ever met.

Unruh could never beat Reagan because Reagan could take his case to the people. Unruh had had enough. Since he couldn't control Reagan, he decided to get rid of him, and the only legal way to do that was to leave the legislature and become Reagan's opponent for the governorship in the 1970 election. It was no contest. Reagan handily defeated *Big Daddy*.

There have been several books written about the leadership skills and qualities of Ronald Reagan. Without attempting to critique what others have already presented, I wish to simply review some personal experiences with Reagan in which he both taught me to understand his leadership style and demonstrated that he knew his responsibility as *the leader of the team*.

In November of 1970, Reagan won re-election to a second term, and it was generally understood that it would be his last. At the beginning of the 1971 calendar year I was elected by my Republican colleagues in the senate as their caucus chairman. Essentially I was the spokesman in the senate for the governor's legislative program. In this capacity I was now called upon to work with the governor and his principal staff members on a daily basis.

At the beginning of his first term in 1967, Reagan had to deal with the overwhelming problems of an underfunded and over-committed state budget. Therefore, he had sought and signed the largest tax increase in the history of the state. Now the situation was much more stable, and with savings coming in from many of the reforms he had sponsored a surplus existed in the state treasury. Reagan was determined to give this surplus back to the people, and to cut their tax burden back to the minimum amount necessary to finance the state government.

Soon after my election as the caucus chairman, Reagan and I

began a series of meetings together, the purpose of which was to facilitate a more effective and reliable rapport between him and the members of the senate. On Monday, April 12, 1971, the Governor and I went over a very extensive strategic analysis of our goal to have a united and reliable base of support from the Republicans in the senate.

Over the next six months I watched Reagan implement many of the proposals we had reviewed that day. In the process, it soon became apparent to me that Reagan's greatest asset as a leader was his own instinctive ability to create a bond between himself and other individuals, be they old friends or new acquaintances, confirmed allies or resolute opponent.

On many occasions I observed a legislator come to Reagan's office, a legislator who was an outspoken opponent of the Governor's objective or purpose. Frequently, though not always, the legislator would leave feeling the warmth and chemistry of an old friend, and many times ready to support what he or she was formerly determined to oppose. For those who came already sympathetic to the Governor's objectives, they would leave convinced that the entire success of the matter under discussion rested solely upon their shoulders.

After Reagan soundly trounced Jess Unruh in the 1970 gubernatorial race, Unruh was replaced as the assembly speaker by a skillful and effective Democratic leader named Robert Moretti. Moretti came from the same part of Los Angeles County that I represented. We had known each other well for nearly ten years. Unruh had skillfully refined the ability to shackle his fellow Democrats in financial bondage through his ability to put funding into their campaigns. He could then be unyielding in demanding absolute loyalty from the beneficiaries of his largess. Moretti had not had the time to forge the same type of control over his colleagues.

On the senate side, the Democrats were led by a soft spoken

scholastic type from San Diego, Senator Jim Mills. An incurable liberal in philosophy, Mills' style of leadership was even less over-bearing than Moretti's. So, even though they had the majority in both houses, the Democratic leaders were by nature and by experience more malleable than Unruh had been. Reagan sensed that he had a golden opportunity, and he moved skillfully to take advantage of it in every way possible.

It was at this time that I became the caucus chairman of the Republicans in the senate. I was now an active participant in the legislative strategy meetings in the governor's office. Now I was observing the governor at close range in his exercise of leadership skills with both his own party members and with the leadership of the Democrats. It is easiest to describe how skillfully Reagan exercised his leadership skills by reviewing my own experiences as a new member of this inner sanctum.

From the very first day that I arrived in my new position the governor treated me with the same respect and consideration that he exhibited toward the most senior and experienced people on his own staff. When at first I demurred from making comments Reagan would look at me, call me by name, and ask what my thoughts were about the matter under discussion. As time passed I became more comfortable in expressing my own views, and he was always the perfect listener. There was direct eye to eye contact, he asked ques-tions that demonstrated he was listening, and he would frequently smile and say something to the effect, "…that makes a lot of sense."

I learned early on that he wanted the participants in these meet-ings to be candid because he was interested in hearing all sides of the issue. Until he made his decision, the participants were free to be as emphatic and energized in defense of the positions as they wanted to be. I have never been with an executive who was more skillful in obtaining the maximum contribution from each individual member of a group than Governor Reagan. At the same time, once he had made his decision he did not appreciate being asked to go back to the issue unless there was some new information that had not previously been discussed. He was always pushing to move on to the next subject.

In 1971 Reagan sent to the legislature a tax reform bill that would return a significant amount of the state surplus to the taxpayers and also lessen the tax burden upon them. By this time in the legislative session (late summer and early fall) resistance to the Reagan charm by the opposition leadership began to harden. Both Moretti and Mills had men under them who were much more contentious than they were. In order to maintain their leadership positions, Moretti and Mills had to dig in their own heels and harden the barriers to what Reagan wanted. In both houses the taxation committee chairmen were under their control, and through this means the Reagan tax reform plan was bogged down.

During the month of October I spent as much as fifteen hours a day in the capitol. In addition to the legislative reapportionment mentioned in chapter one the enactment of the governor's tax reform measure was drawing fire. On Wednesday, October 27, Reagan met in his office with the entire legislative leadership, both Republicans and Democrats. For an hour he negotiated directly with Moretti and Mills and their respective associates for some commitment that they would stop stonewalling his tax reform measure and let the legislature vote directly on the merits. Both men knew that we had the votes in both houses if we could only get the bills to the respective floors for a vote.

After the Democrats left, Reagan and his principal staff people met with us, the Republican leadership. We examined a variety of options, discussing where the resistance might be weakest and how we could exploit that to secure passage of the bill. Finally Reagan made a pivotal decision.

"I'm going to take my case to the people of the state," he said. "I know I can get them to support us." Reagan, as usual, knew exactly what he wanted to get and now resolved how he would get it.

He initiated a series of speaking engagements up and down the state. Slowly at first and then like an avalanche, the momentum in support of Reagan's proposal became huge. I had members of the senate from the Democratic side come to me and say, "…tell the governor he has my vote, just get his people in my district off my back." The Reagan tax reform bill passed, and the surplus was given back to the taxpayers. Many pseudo-political scientists have dismissed this event as only a minor and momentary change of direction, and not nearly as significant a victory as Reagan and his supporters have described it.

But it was an incredible victory and deserves to be understood as one of the most compelling demonstrations of Reagan's leadership ability. He did in fact reverse a supposedly irreversible appetite on the part of the state for more and more money. At that time California's annual budget was the eighth largest government budget in the world, let alone the largest among the fifty states. There were programs for spending coming from every conceivable source. Bureaucrats along with elected officials had no problem bringing in massive spending concepts. The teacher's union in the state was constantly at our doors promising university scholarships for every high school dropout if we would only give them more money and let them spend it the way they wanted.

Reagan could have accepted many of these proposals, among them many that were indeed meritorious and appealing. But he knew that there was no end to what could be dreamed up to spend all of the people's money, and put the state right back in the hole it was in when he became governor. He also knew that there were other ways, much better ways, to achieve many of these goals and objectives. For a man who was constantly being promoted as a presidential candidate, the temptation to accept many of these proposals and to use them for his own political enhancement might have seemed irresistible. Reagan never faltered, however, and never allowed himself to be seduced by the promise of personal political benefit if he would only allow these spending programs to go forward. Reagan's integrity and honor, which were really the secret to his capacity as a leader, were never more clearly demonstrated than in that 1971 legislative session.

On Wednesday, March 1, 1972, I participated in a luncheon meeting with Reagan, which also included other legislative leaders and members of his staff. These luncheon meetings were held frequently, depending on the governor's schedule and other factors. At this particular luncheon I was seated next to Reagan. Whether that was by design or accident I cannot say. The reason it is so memorable is because he spent most of the time, while others were eating, visiting with me about our relationship.

I have noted elsewhere the expressions of frustration from both Robert Finch and also Ed Reinecke, who at this time was still Reagan's lieutenant governor, about their personal relationships with Reagan. Given the difference in our ages and our circumstances, it never occurred to me to presume to have what could be considered a personal social relationship with the Reagans. Yet, often in the course of our professional relationship we became engaged in highly personal conversations. This happened to be one of those occasions which is why it is so vivid in my memory.

"Our relationship has gone through some stormy periods, hasn't it?" he said, turning to me as we were eating lunch. My immediate reaction was to wonder whether someone had said I was unhappy about some matter involving Reagan and the senate. My response was to simply dismiss the thought that there was any reason to be concerned about my loyalty to him or my appreciation for his leadership.

"I understand that," he said. "I just wanted you to know that I realize we have not always agreed on things but you have never let that interfere with doing your best for me in the senate. I want you to know how much I appreciate that."

As our discussion continued he was as gracious and open as anyone could have desired. Yet, not withstanding the warmth of the conversation, there remained something almost regal about his demeanor and his presence that made it inappropriate to become too familiar. As I returned to my office there was a very distinct sense of re-commitment on my part to support Reagan in whatever way I could. The leader had taken a few minutes to strengthen the loyalty of one of his lieutenants. He had been spectacularly effective, and by so doing had confirmed that he had no need to worry about my labors on his behalf.

A variety of other occasions also served to demonstrate his leadership ability and, at the same time, some of the principles that he applied in his relationship with subordinates. As his chief of staff, Ed Meese noted,

"Reagan extended to his staff members the same right to have and enjoy their privacy that he wanted for himself. He wanted his staff people to protect their personal lives from disruption by the constant sense of urgency that attends senior government officials. He was most reluctant to personally intrude into the private time of his principal staff members. If necessary, they were free to call him, but seldom did he feel that a situation merited his intruding into their evenings or weekends. He would frequently inquire about family members and when he found a staff member consistently remaining late in the office he would take the time for a private visit in which he would express his concern that this person's personal and family life were suffering because of commitment to the work at hand."

But Reagan's sensitivity to his staff and others did not prevent him from exercising more visible forms of leadership in which tough decisions were made and tough people were given to understand that the governor was no *patsy*. On one occasion one of the senior Democrats in the senate made it clear to Reagan that unless the governor accepted an amendment to a proposed welfare reform bill it would never clear his committee. Reagan's response was equally clear and unequivocal. Calling the senator by his first name, and with a slight smile, Reagan responded, "…we will just have to put on the gloves over this one, won't we." The bill later cleared the committee, against the chairman's opposition. The other members of the committee had no desire to have Reagan campaigning against them in their districts.

There were several members of the Republican senate delegation who made an art of forcing me to use every stratagem possible to assure their support for a critical vote on behalf of the administration. Frequently I had to spend one half of my time with just two or three of the nineteen or twenty Republican members of the senate.

On one occasion I was having a particularly difficult time with one of these individuals, a man whose loyalty to anything or anyone was constantly being changed by the skillful use of favors or financial support. I finally arranged a meeting between this senator and the governor in order to let the senator personally tell the governor what his price would be for supporting the matter to be voted on.

The tone and content of the meeting was cordial and respectful, but Reagan did not want to make the particular promise or commitment that my colleague was seeking from him. Reagan was careful not to offend the man, and did not simply refuse to consider the request. Reagan simply assured this shameless chameleon that his request would be "…kept in mind." When the man departed, the governor gave me some advice and an insight into his capacity to evaluate individuals.

"John, don't waste your time with him," he said. "People like that are never worthy of your efforts. They have no sense of dignity nor any guiding principles. You can never rely on someone for whom expedience is the only criteria for a decision."

This comment brought into sharp focus the difference in character between Ronald Reagan and the individual who had just left. For Reagan, principle and integrity were everything. No matter what the most opportune thing to do might have been, the governor remained steadfast to that unwritten but prevailing set of principles which guided his decisions.

On many other occasions I saw Reagan demonstrate his ability to discern the nature of an individual's commitment to principle. While Reagan was a partisan in many ways, his partisanship was never allowed to distort his measure of an individual's essential character. There were many in the opposing political party for whom he had genuine respect and appreciation because, though they differed, the difference was founded on genuine belief in principle and not on expediency or the political exploitation of others. However, whenever Reagan saw what he thought was the exploitation of the people by those in the government, particularly the use of welfare programs or transfer payments to buy the support of a particular segment of society, his disgust for such abuse of the political process was very evident.

In my position as the Republican caucus chairman I needed to have Reagan's assistance in fund raising events for the Republican state senators and our non-incumbent candidates. He was always willing to accommodate those requests. Again, it reflected his clear perception of his responsibility as the leader, and also displayed his skill in fulfilling that responsibility.

I would meet with Reagan, then having obtained his commitment for a particular event, would proceed to develop and organize the details. He never failed to put forth all of the effort at his command to make these events successful financially and personally for the candidate or candidates involved. He never asked to be relieved of this burden. There was no effective substitute for a Ronald Reagan personal appearance.

Reagan had about him a cadre of men outside of government whose loyalty to him was a powerful testimony of his leadership capacity. These individuals were referred to as the "kitchen cabinet," and the magnitude of their individual accomplishments was awe inspiring. These were men who in business and finance had dealt with tremendous challenges and had been able to acquire the material means and the personal capacity to make things happen that others considered difficult or impossible. They remained a vital part of the Reagan phenomenon for more than twenty-five years. Had Ronald Reagan not actually been what he seemed to be on camera, most if not all of these men would never have remained so loyal to him.

During fund raising efforts on behalf of my colleagues, I worked closely with many of these individuals. While many could be mentioned, I shall resist the desire to discuss the more than twenty individual members of Reagan's "kitchen cabinet" whose names are in my journals, and refer here to just four of them: Holmes Tuttle, "Jack" Hulme, Ed Mills, and Richard "Dick" Gulbranson. Jack Hulme was headquartered in the San Francisco bay area, the others in southern California.

Each of these men was characterized by loyalty to Ronald Reagan. All of them had frequent opportunity to see him in private moments. On one occasion Reagan and I were driving together to a meeting and he began to talk about Ed Mills and Dick Gulbranson. He was profoundly aware of the hundreds of hours these two men were spending on his behalf, and on behalf of the Republican party.

He spoke with genuine awe for their sacrifice and their constant loyalty. He spoke with very real emotion of the fact that he could never adequately thank them or compensate them for what they were doing in their respective responsibilities. Then he made one of those reflective comments that would come with no warning but which zeroed in on the essence of Ronald Reagan's personal philosophy.

"You know," he said, "Ed and Dick are the quintessential examples of what makes America great, and of what will keep America the greatest nation on earth. As long as we can produce men like Ed Mills and Dick Gulbranson, as long as our nation has men and women of this caliber willing and able to make personal sacrifice for our national heritage and future, we will not only survive but grow ever stronger."

It was also reflective of Reagan as a leader that such individuals were so willing to follow him. People like these sensed in Reagan the qualities they valued in their own lives. They were indeed kindred spirits, and the bonds between them were deeper than seeking social status or the amenities of political power. These were men and women who knew instinctively that here was a giant of a man who had the capacity to give powerful, inspired, and honorable leadership to the state and the nation in an hour of need. To work with such a man, for however little or long, for whatever personal sacrifice was required, was an opportunity to participate in something destined to bless future generations. In some way, the Reagan legacy to America and her future generations would be their legacy as well.

Ed Meese shared with me some insights into Reagan's preparations to begin his first term as president. When the issue of the appointments to the president's cabinet came up in 1980, Reagan set five criteria that he wanted to use in measuring the desirability of any potential cabinet appointee:

A. Loyalty to the President

B. Integrity

C. Competence, experience, and intellectual capability

D. Not having an "agenda" of their own

E. Have the "toughness" to deal with the media, the bureaucracy, the congress, etc.

These were his ideas of what he wanted. In selecting men and women for his administration he assiduously followed this agenda. He wanted to have around him men and women who would be loyal to him, yet he did not want to have obsequious puppets who had no will or vision of their own. As governor Reagan had utilized these same criteria, which was why he was consistently able to convince high performance individuals to leave exceptional situations of prestige and income to join his administration.

Reagan's style as the president was simply an extension of the way in which he dealt with things in Sacramento. As Governor he often would say, "…let's round table this with some of the fellows." By that he meant that before a decision was made on something he wanted to get feedback from those whom he had chosen to work with him as governor. No one individual had a decision making monopoly on any particular aspect of state government. Reagan worked hard to have talented people around him, and he insisted that this collective brain power be used to analyze the issues that were being resolved in his office.

Reagan had the habit in Sacramento of going to the offices of the various state agencies to hold cabinet meetings so that he and others in the cabinet could get a feel for how the various departments of state government worked. On at least two occasions when the issues before him required some on-the-spot inspection he took the cabinet on horseback into Round Valley and to the area where the Disney

Corporation wanted to build a nature theme park. Often when an issue to be decided involved a particular location in the state he would schedule a personal visit and would request those responsible to accompany him.

Reagan's skill as a leader became apparent in other ways as well. On one occasion there was an intense confrontation between the Republican legislative leadership and Reagan's senior staff. We were meeting with the governor in his small working office, and individuals were seated close enough to each other to make it unnecessary to speak loudly. Nonetheless, the decibel range for several individual's voices was going off the chart. The tension and the intensity of feeling in the room became very high. Reagan, who was sitting at his desk, reached for the jelly bean jar, took several jelly beans, and then passed them around the room. By the time the jelly bean jar had gotten back to his desk tempers were under control and emotions were subdued sufficiently to allow the situation to be dealt with in a more dignified manner. Reagan had not spoken a word, but he had effectively maintained control over a situation that was dangerously close to getting out of hand.

A final example of his leadership skills and how he honed them in preparation for the presidency was his relationship with other governors. He enjoyed the governor's conferences, although he once commented that he felt there was too much social activity and not enough working sessions.

What amazed his peers at his first governor's conference was his ability to participate in panel discussions regarding regional problems with very specific knowledge of the issues involved and very specific recommendations as to how to deal with them. Many of the other governors had come to the conference having been misled by the media into believing that Reagan's political success was a function of the skillful campaign strategists around him. They were not prepared for the reality that here was a man fully capable of absorbing, recalling, and skillfully communicating the specific details of those regional and national issues which were on the agenda. Once he had studied something he could retain what he had read and could assimilate it with his own ideas.

Reagan was the host for the governor's conference in 1968 when Nixon came as the president-elect. There were thirty one or thirty two Republican governors. Ed Meese noted that Reagan personally oversaw the details for the planning of the conference. He was determined that the conference would be a very productive experience for the governors in which they would deal in depth with relevant issues. In the words of Paul Laxalt, then governor of Nevada, "Reagan put on a great conference." Again Ed Meese noted that Reagan obviously enjoyed the other governors and got along well with them. A final testimonial to his leadership skills is the fact that many of his most enthusiastic supporters for the presidency were governors who had first met him at these conferences.

FOUR

COURAGE & STRENGTH

Every Wednesday that the California legislature was in session, from 1966 through 1975, a group of the governmental affairs representatives (lobbyists) of various California industrial associations, corporations and public entities, would jointly host a luncheon for the members of the state senate. Some of our hosts were men who had been on the scene in Sacramento for more than twenty-five years. Many of them went back to the days of Earl Warren's first administration. These Wednesday luncheons were a marvelous learning experience for a young state senator like me. I listened attentively to the various anecdotes about governors and legislators who had left a great legacy in Sacramento.

In February of 1967 Reagan was in his second month of his first term as governor. As his new administration came together, the governmental affairs representatives were very curious to know about the people Reagan was bringing to Sacramento with him. After the election, but before the inauguration, these oftentimes cynical and self assured *old hands* were asking themselves how this total neophyte to the complexities of government could hope to manage the largest state of the union.

Who would Reagan get to take the various positions in his cabinet? Who would be his director of finance? How would this former actor be able to attract individuals with enough political savvy to give his administration the skill necessary to deal with a legislature that was dominated by the opposite party in both houses?

Reagan demonstrated very quickly that he intended to staff his administration with the most capable individuals he could find. It wasn't long until the old Sacramento hands were scratching their heads, and commenting with genuine awe that no governor in this century had been able to attract the caliber of men Reagan was bringing to Sacramento. Day after day the governor's office would announce a new appointment of someone who was taking a dramatic cut in pay or even an uncompensated leave of absence in order to come and be a part of the Reagan administration.

At one of these Wednesday luncheons I sat beside two of these old Sacramento hands. They were commenting about Gordon Paul Smith, Reagan's director of finance, and Gordon Luce, the secretary of the Department of Business and Transportation. These were men worthy of presidential appointments in Washington.

"How does he do it?" they would ask me. I had no idea, but decided to see if I could find out.

I went to Reagan's legislative liaison with the state assembly, Jack Lindsey. He was one of the people the old hands were asking about. A successful business executive with a great future in a California food company, he had agreed to take a two-year leave of absence to join Reagan in Sacramento. Lindsey, like most of the other appointees, was no political hack. He had not spent years in the political process working his way up through the party chairs so that he could get an appointive office. Like so many of those whom Reagan attracted to his side, Lindsey was a leader, an effective administrator, and took a significant cut in pay to join the Reagan team. When Jack left Sacramento to return to his business career I heard the Democratic speaker of the state assembly, Jesse Unruh, say,

"Reagan has no idea what he owes to this man. He got me to

agree to things that I should never have let Reagan obtain. Lindsey deserves an appointment to the state Supreme Court."

This was the ultimate political compliment for a man who was not a lawyer, coming from a man who was already preparing to run against Reagan in the 1970 election. Unruh was acknowledging that Lindsey's negotiating skills were superior or at least equal to any he had dealt with before.

I asked Lindsey what Reagan did to get these people. Jack described the process as follows:

"First, the governor gets a clear picture of the responsibilities that will be placed upon the person in the particular position under discussion. Then he asks for a list of individuals whose current executive and administrative experience makes them qualified for the task, regardless of political background or party affiliation.

"The governor discusses the list with his senior staff members. He will often make a phone call or two to other individuals personally acquainted with the people on the list. Finally, he will select two or three of those on the list to call and talk to personally.

"When Reagan has found the person he thinks he wants to select, he places a telephone call to that individual and asks him to come to Sacramento, or to set a time and place mutually convenient when they can meet. Then, the magic of the Reagan personality comes through. Invariably the candidate begins by making it clear that he does not think he can afford to leave his present situation for a stint of public service in Sacramento. The idea of moving his family, of taking a leave of absence from his business or professional situation, '… is just not practical.'

"Reagan then talks a little about the critical challenges facing the state, and of his intense desire to bring high-performance individuals into key administrative positions in the government. Finally, he tells a few stories, and then when a level of rapport has been reached that he feels is what he needs, he closes the deal."

"You make it sound almost theatrical," I said.

"No, " Lindsey said, "Not theatrical. I'm describing strong executive leadership. When these individuals meet with Reagan they can sense his courage and his strength of character. Reagan is a man who can inspire other men to want to join him in a noble cause."

Whatever the source of his courage may have been, Ronald Reagan never was afraid to stand alone. On hundreds of occasions during our eight years together I watched him deal with intense challenges. It was particularly impressive to me that on those occasions when those about him were advocating a course of action that was different from what he knew to be right, he would quietly, but with evident inner strength, make it clear he would proceed on the path that conscience and principle required him to follow.

Reagan never wilted in the heat of opposition. He seemed to actually draw strength from the ridicule and contempt of those who demeaned his convictions. It didn't matter if he were in a press conference with thirty or forty critical and often rude media people and a dozen television cameras, in front of a gathering of legislators, or in an auditorium with a thousand people who had been recruited and trained to disrupt his talk and heckle him, the reaction was always the same. He maintained a sense of authority, an air of confidence in himself and what he intended to accomplish. His courage and conviction never wavered.

Reagan's physical bearing as he entered a room was never the swagger of a bully, yet he walked with an air of strength. When working with him in the governor's office, one felt the vibrations of conviction that seemed to radiate from his entire being. I have read the accounts of people who had interviews with Reagan and who depicted him as mumbling and uncertain, literally out of touch with reality. Nothing could be farther from the truth, based on my work and interaction with him in Sacramento. During the time of his presidency I watched from a distance and saw how the burden of the office weighed heavy on his countenance, but I never saw any evidence at any time that the intellectual and physical vitality, so evident in California, had slipped away.

In his first term as governor, Reagan followed a pattern of weekly press conferences. From the beginning Reagan's press conferences were standing room only occasions. It was not my habit to attend these meetings with the press, although I did sit in on several of them to make certain that I knew what both the media and the governor considered to be the critical issues of the day. The media fascination with Reagan was always interesting to watch. Whatever the majority of the working press may have thought about his philosophy, or about him personally, they didn't let these attitudes keep them from doing everything possible to exploit the public interest in Reagan as a means of selling their wares.

On Tuesday, July 9, 1968, Reagan held an especially important press conference. At issue was the matter of the state budget deficit, with which Reagan had been wrestling since coming to office. Former Governor Pat Brown and the liberal-dominated legislature had obligated the state to a variety of social welfare programs that could not possibly be financed out of the existing revenue base.

I was invited to the press conference because I had emerged as one of the more visible spokesmen for the conservative members of the senate. I had taken the public position that these programs, particularly the Medi-Cal program, had to be revised from top to bottom before any more funding could be justified. Inasmuch as the governor was about to announce that he would be asking for the largest tax increase in the history of the state, Reagan and his staff did not want to risk a public fight with the conservative members of his own party. At least they wanted to be certain that we understood his position before taking a public stance against any tax increase.

Reagan had campaigned with a promise to cut the size and cost of California's government. The persuasiveness of his message of *cut, squeeze, and trim* the state budget gave him a margin of victory over Pat Brown of more than a million votes. Now he was announcing the largest tax increase in the history of the state. Those in the media who were waiting for a chance to ambush this *has-been movie cowboy*, as they referred to him in their personal conversations, were rubbing their hands in glee, thinking they finally had *Ronnie* in a corner.

When Reagan entered the room there was an almost electric sensation among those present. The working press are a very callused and cynical lot, often inclined to denigrate those who have a genuinely passionate devotion to principles founded on individual liberty and the preservation of our constitutional heritage. But even those of the media who were contemptuous of all that Reagan believed and espoused could not conceal their fascination with the power of his personality. When he entered the press conference room even those of the media most determined to depict Reagan as a *former B-movie actor with little or no capacity to govern* could not deny his dominating presence.

From start to finish Reagan was master of the moment. He was candid in his admission that this decision was an apparent repudiation of his campaign promises. Yet he was not cowed into any words of concession suggesting he was not still committed to those objectives and promises which won him the election. His body language was still very much that of the leader, though suffering a temporary setback. He was not defeated or in retreat. He quipped "...the cracking you hear is the concrete breaking from around my feet. I was determined never to come to this moment, but it is here, and has to be dealt with."

The real test came in the question and answer session. The cynics and the arrogant bore down with question after question that was supposed to knock the *cowboy* out of the saddle. None of it worked. He kept his composure, responding with specific detail to the issues that were raised and he never lost the aura of confidence that was so much his trademark. His head may have been temporarily bloodied, but it was not bowed.

Ed Meese shared with me some of the more memorable moments in the White House when others were convinced that certain disaster awaited Reagan if he continued to pursue a particular course.

"He would not allow American businesses to provide the Soviets those things that would enhance their economy," Meese said, "because it would increase their ability to finance their military growth." A lot of American companies pressured him to let them sell to the Soviets the equipment to enhance their oil and gas production. He refused to do that, even though he knew the Soviets could get this material from other countries. "At least we won't make it easy for them," he said.

On a number of occasions very powerful business executives were furious that Reagan refused to budge from this position. Clearly they were in a position to mobilize significant financial and personal resources against Reagan. But Meese said,

"Reagan was unwavering in his determination that the Soviets not be given anything that would enhance their ability to continue with the Cold War. Reagan understood the significant importance of economics in pressuring the Soviet's into peaceful negotiations. Because of his courage and strength of conviction throughout those eight years that is exactly what happened."

When I asked Meese for examples of Reagan's determination to win the Cold War from the White House period, he cited the following:

1. The speech Reagan made to the British parliament in 1982, in which he said that in a time soon to come *'communism would be consigned to the ash heap of history.'*

2. The speech to the evangelical Christians in 1983, in which Reagan depicted the Soviet Union as *'the evil empire.'*

3. The Brandenburg Gate speech at the Berlin Wall in 1987, when he publicly challenged Gorbechev to *"...take down this wall."*

4. The speech at the University of Moscow in 1988, in which he committed the United States to never waver from its position of defending individual liberty and free agency.

It may be difficult for those who are thirty years removed from the dynamics of the Cold War to understand the extent of inner courage and conviction required for Ronald Reagan to refuse to be intimidated from his chosen course by those voices of doubt and criticism. These were the electronic media pundits, the congressional oracles who believed that they alone possessed the wisdom and the experience to govern the nation, the editorial page writers and the pseudo-intellectuals who knew all the answers but never had to produce any results. These were the voices of despair who continued to warn that Reagan's policies would lead the nation to the fearful nuclear holocaust of which they spoke so much but knew so little.

Reagan paid little heed to them. With certainty of purpose he stood firm in his conviction that with the strength of freedom's creative power this nation could lead the world to a better day. That day ultimately dawned, in large part because a man named Ronald Reagan had the courage and strength to wield the sword of truth in defense of liberty and freedom.

FIVE

VIRTUE & DIGNITY

For years people have been asking me questions about Ronald Reagan. The questions are phrased in different ways, but invariably there is one basic issue that always seems to come up. Was Ronald Reagan really who and what he seemed to be? Was the image he portrayed the real man? Can you assure me that what I have believed about him is true?

As I have pondered these questions and attempted to answer them I have tried to understand what it is that people are really asking. Why is it that they are so anxious to be assured that what they saw in Ronald Reagan was genuine?

In order to answer that question I first had to understand what it was they saw in him. What was he at his inner core?

Since the 1950s there seems to be an accelerating decline in the values and mores of the American people. That which was once deemed vulgar and offensive is now gaudily paraded in our arts and media. That which was once shunned as indecent and vile, unsuitable among any group of refined or cultured people is now commonplace in our colleges and universities. Once we were a nation of sensitive and kindly people. Now violence and aggressive hostility are found in nearly every sphere of our lives, from the freeway to the neighborhood grocery store.

The last half of the twentieth century was a time of such remarkable change that foreigners once familiar with the American character commented that they can find no one and nothing in our culture that once instilled such hope among other peoples.

In her novel on the life of Cicero, *A Pillar of Iron*, author Taylor Caldwell quotes Cicero as making the following commentary on the moral decadence into which the Roman Empire had descended.

> *The daily spectacle of atrocious acts has stifled all feeling of pity in the hearts of men. When every hour we see or hear of an act of dreadful cruelty we lose all feeling of humanity. Crime no longer horrifies us. We smile at the enormities of our youth. We condone passion, when we should understand that the unrestrained emotions of man produce chaos.*
>
> *Once we were a nation of self-control and austerity, and had a reverence of life and justice. This is no longer true. We prefer our politicians, particularly if they swagger with youth and are accomplished jesters and liars. We love entertainment, even in law, even in government. Unless we reform our fate is terrible.*
>
> *A Pillar of Iron*, Caldwell, p. 322

What Cicero depicted in the early decline of Roman civilization now defines what has happened to America in the last half of the twentieth century. Ronald Reagan awakened among the American people an awareness of the America they once knew. The America of their parents and grandparents was a nation of people who were, in the classical sense of that word, virtuous. According to *Family Word Finder* published by *Reader's Digest* in 1975, a virtuous people are upright, honorable, high-principled; ethical, just, meritorious, praiseworthy, commendable, laudable, exemplary. In the totality of that definition, Ronald Reagan was a virtuous man.

Those questions asked by members of every audience in the

hundreds of appearances that I made on behalf of or about Ronald Reagan, were really asking for the assurance that he truly was a man of virtue and dignity. In answer to that question I gave then an affirmative and absolutely unqualified yes. Ronald Reagan was, in every sense of those two words, a man of virtue and dignity.

The yearning to find someone upon whom the mantle of Ronald Reagan can fall comes from the fact that with his departure the last great symbol of those qualities we call *virtue*, and *dignity*, were gone. We had been proud to have as our nation's president a man who represented the America that had saved the world from Hitler and Stalin. Instinctively people seemed to sense that the new America is only a shadow of what our nation had been as defined by the character of its citizenry. The constant search for another Ronald Reagan is simply a plea to God to raise up in our midst another who is worthy of that mantle.

In Reagan's presence one felt dignity, and that which was common or vulgar was totally inappropriate. Even in the more casual working sessions, or on those rare occasions when he would remove his suit coat and loosen his tie, there was about Ronald Reagan an atmosphere of refinement, of being above the petty and the mundane. If he wanted to increase a sense of unity and harmony in a working group he would rely upon his seemingly endless reserve of humorous stories. With two or three anecdotes, often poking fun at himself, he could create a working atmosphere that was relaxed and open without in any way compromising his sense of dignity and propriety. He never turned to topics that were unsavory or cheap or that demeaned another person or groups of people. If he was critical of an individual or a group the criticism was related directly to the ideas they espoused or the causes in which they were engaged.

On one occasion the Governor invited members of the legislature and their wives to his home for an evening that included being entertained by a famous Hollywood personality, Jack Benney. His presentation included a series of *off color* stories which seemed out of character for him, but may have been motivated by his prior experiences with politicians. Whatever the reason, my wife and I were sitting close enough to Governor and Mrs. Reagan that I could easily discern their discomfort with that part of the program. Though Reagan was the host, and the performer was both a long time friend and a famous entertainer, Reagan's countenance and demeanor did not respond approvingly to the presentation. I realized then that in all my opportunities to be with him and on all of the occasions when he would use humor as a means of achieving some present objective in the discussion, I could never remember him saying anything that I would not want to share with my wife and children.

Reagan had a great sense of personal responsibility to honor by word and action the office to which he had been elected. As governor, and later as president, he exemplified the highest qualities of personal conduct and demeanor. That was for him a significant part of fulfilling the mandate that had been given to him by the people. Ed Meese recalls that as president, Reagan would never remove his coat while in the Oval Office, because of the reverence he had for that historic place.

On one occasion I remember Reagan's sense of formality going too far. During one of his campaigns the campaign staff wanted some photos of Reagan out at the ranch riding his horse. Reagan appeared at the appointed hour attired in formal riding breeches and knee high leather boots. Lyn Nofiziger had to send him back into the house to put on his levis and cowboy boots, which Reagan had in abundance, but which he associated with his physical labor on the ranch but not suitable for the office of governor. He was finally persuaded that in this instance there would be no danger of lessening the dignity of the office by wearing old levis and scruffy cowboy boots.

This attitude of reverence for the dignity of the office was not contrived or artificial. He made it unequivocally clear that he felt that he owed the highest standard of dignity in word and action to the people of California as their governor.

On one or two rare occasions when confronted by an individual or group whose language and hostility had exceeded common decency, Reagan might momentarily step off the pedestal. After all, Reagan, as he often reminded us, was Irish. On one occasion I met with him immediately after his return from a meeting of the regents of the University of California. The Governor was accosted by a group of the campus militants whose obscene language and vulgar placards revealed their back-alley morals and mentality. Barely audible and with tight lips Reagan *vented* his feelings, regretting that the taxpayers of California, who were paying for the education of such individuals, were not getting a suitable return on their investment.

Ed Meese was a close observer of the various efforts to "stage" Reagan in a certain way. "He was never really comfortable with much of that business," Meese said. "He wanted to be perceived as he was, not as something he was not. He was very comfortable with himself and was confident that who and what he was in reality needed no artificial frosting in order to make him more heroic in the eyes of the public."

Meese shared with me a very private experience with Reagan in Sacramento that revealed both his sense of personal virtue and the bond of unity and loyalty that he felt for Nancy. The Governor and Meese, with several other staff people, came out of the Sutter Club in Sacramento where they had participated in a luncheon meeting that included several senior legislators. A comment was made about the girlfriend of one of the married legislators. As they walked back to the capitol, Reagan said to Meese, "You know, I could never do that.

Nancy would know."

He was simply noting that she would know because of the nature of their relationship. The bond between them was pure and without compromise. Reagan knew that if he said or did anything inconsistent with that commitment Nancy would sense that something was wrong. Ronald Reagan's fundamental integrity was such that for the people he served, and for his own beloved companion, there was total loyalty and fidelity. He was not willing to compromise that commitment.

During 1972 I had a variety of occasions to talk with Governor Reagan about his own concerns about public morality and virtue. The basis for those discussions was a state-wide anti-pornography ballot initiative. I was the author and principal sponsor.

The California constitution provides that under certain conditions the people themselves may enact statutory provisions or make changes to the state constitution when the legislature will not. The process includes obtaining a certain number of signatures of duly registered voters on petitions which contain the proposed statutory language. These petitions need to be presented to the chief election officer of the state, the secretary of state, who after validating the signatures as being those of registered voters, will then place the proposed statute on the next ballot.

In 1972 in California, with one tenth of the entire American population living within the state, an initiative petition needed over one million valid signatures in order to qualify for the ballot. The usual ratio of valid to invalid signatures was two to one, meaning that it was necessary to get three signatures in order to get two that qualified. The time ordinarily required to collect a sufficient number of valid signatures was eight months to a year, or even longer. The cost usually came to about a dollar per signature, or at least a million dollars.

In what is still regarded as one of the most remarkable achievements in the history of California's political processes, I decided to take to the people of the state an initiative petition that would substantially strengthen the ability of local prosecutors and law enforcement officials to deal with the production and distribution of pornography. In order to qualify for the November 1972 ballot, we obtained over a million qualified signatures of registered voters in less than a month. Our initiative was able to be included on the ballot for November of 1972. It was called *Proposition 18.*

As this process unfolded I had various conversations with Governor Reagan about the content of the legislative package. The pro pornography Motion Picture Producer's Association was slowly but effectively defeating the bills as our legislation moved through the legislative process. Ordinarily, the Governor did not endorse legislation that didn't originate in his office until after it was passed. He never knew what changes the legislature might make in any given piece of legislation that could make it inappropriate for the Governor to endorse it. However, Reagan was very supportive of what I was attempting to accomplish and was always interested in my progress reports.

When we accomplished the miracle of qualifying for the November 1972 ballot in an impossibly short period of time, Reagan called to congratulate me. Later that day, at the end of a meeting with other legislative leaders, I remained behind to ask if he would be willingly to publicly endorse *Proposition 18.* There was no hesitancy in his reply. "Absolutely," he said. "You have my endorsement, and my prayers for your success."

On the day that he agreed to endorse *Proposition 18,* I described to him the content of some of the material being produced and distributed in California by the pornography industry. Several times as we were talking he would grimace and would shake his head from side to side in disbelief. During the conversation he doubled up his fist and slowly brought it down upon his desk. He had not spoken a word, but there was no doubt as to how he felt about this sordid material.

Between then and the November election we had various opportunities to discuss the campaign for *Proposition 18*. This was before the internet, which now can bring pornography into most every home. In 1972 the primary outlet for visual pornography was the adult movie theater. The Motion Picture Producer's Association (MPPA) helped finance the defense of the pornography industry. The American Civil Liberties Union (ACLU) constantly provided legal assistance to the pornographers. Reagan shared with me his own distress at the rapidly increasing amount of graphic sex and violence in motion pictures. He minced no words about the ruthlessness of the individuals who ran the MPPA.

"They lie, and use all of the power at their command to crush anyone who dares question their conduct," he said. "No one in the movie business dares to cross them. Watch your backside," he said, "for there is nothing they will not do to put down a threat to their own power."

I was startled at the intensity with which he condemned the very industry where he had once worked. He saw the reaction in my countenance to what he had said, and he offered this brief further explanation.

"John, there was a day when Hollywood represented all that made America so great. We extolled good over evil, right over wrong, and truth over error. We entertained in a manner that could make people forget their troubles, and give them assurance of a better world and a brighter tomorrow. When someone was down and needed an emotional lift or a sense of renewed hope there was a motion picture close by to provide that. But that is no longer the way Hollywood works. Now, it is a matter of exploiting the bizarre, the violent, the dark side of human behavior and nature. Your proposition is badly needed," he said, "and you have my unqualified endorsement."

Reagan was true to his word. He approved a statement in favor of the proposition. He allowed his photograph to be used in our literature in support of the measure. He and I recorded a radio endorsement of *Proposition 18,* but sadly, there was never sufficient funding to put it on the air.

Whenever we came together that summer and fall he would inquire as to how we were doing. Usually we were optimistic, but as election day drew closer and the incredible financial power of the MPPA was unleashed in a tidal wave of misrepresentation and distortion, our base of support began to wither. When the election was over, and we had lost by a two-to-one margin, Reagan offered his regrets. "I hope you won't give up the fight," he said. "What you are doing is right, and it needs to be done."

Within a few months the subject of *Proposition 18* was again a matter of lengthy discussion between us, but for a different reason. Reagan was determined to take to the people of California a constitutional amendment that would limit the percentage of the gross annual product of the state that the state government could take in taxes. In order to get it on the ballot he needed to accomplish the same thing that we did in terms of gathering signatures. Fortunately for him he had more time, money, and support for his endeavor. Unfortunately, a tactical decision on the timing of the election doomed his effort.

The virtue and dignity of Ronald Reagan is embodied in the following quotation by Plutarch, the Greek biographer and essayist, who after having studied the lives of many important Greek and Roman governors, wrote the following:

"Men, steered by popular applause, though they bear the names of governors, are in reality the mere underlings of the multitude. The man who is completely wise and virtuous has no need at all for glory, except so far as it disposes and eases his way of action by the greater trust that it procures him."

Bartlett's Familiar Quotations,
13th and Centennial Edition, page 57.

It is well known that one of Ronald Reagan's favorite axioms was:

There is no end to the good that can be accomplished if you do not worry about who gets the credit.

He was genuinely uninterested in getting the credit. He accepted public adulation as a necessary part of his public service. Michael Deaver, the Governor's principal image maker, often experienced frustration at Reagan's seeming lack of interest in staged situations intended to add a greater air of heroism to Reagan's public image. His disregard for self-promotion raised the question of how he came to be twice elected as the governor of the nation's most populous state, and twice elected as president.

There is a remarkable degree of similarity between the situation in California, when Ronald Reagan was first elected governor, and the circumstances in 1980, when he was first elected president. On both occasions there seemed to be a public awareness that something was wrong. The mood of the electorate on both occasions was one of intense concern for the ship of state. California in 1966 was struggling with the burden of unfunded state programs. In 1980 the national attitude has moved from a state of "malaise," to use the words of then President Jimmy Carter, to one of great alarm over double digit interest rates on home mortgages (as high as twenty-one percent) and the renewed specter of runaway inflation.

Edward Everett, in his *Mount Vernon Papers # 14*, analyzed this phenomenon of how the American people, when faced with such a tough situation, seemed to instinctively come back to politics in an effort to put someone in charge who had the virtue and integrity to resolve the situation. He said:

> *The days of balmy prosperity are not those most favorable to the display of public virtue or the influence of wise and good men. In hard, doubtful, unprosperous and dangerous times, the disinterested and patriotic find their way, by a species of public instinct, unopposed, joyfully welcomed, to the control of affairs.*
> *Bartlett's Familiar Quotations*, 13th Edition, pp 471-472.

Thus it was that in 1966, and again in 1980, the disinterested and patriotic people of California and the nation, sensing that these were doubtful and dangerous times, came back to the polling booth to take control of affairs and place into the office of the chief executive, one who was possessed of virtue and dignity. Under the leadership of that man, the ship of state was placed once more on a direct course leading to a harbor of safety.

SIX

VISION & ACTION
A MAN WHO STOOD ALONE

On January 2nd, 1967, I was one of nearly a thousand people who stood watching Ronald Reagan take the oath of office as the thirty-third governor of California. We had attended the inaugural ball, during which I met another Reagan who would become a classic icon in my life, the older brother to our new governor, Neil "Moon" Reagan. During the next few weeks the Reagan team became accustomed to their offices, and I, as the youngest member of the state senate, began my educational process in the relationship between the executive and legislative branches of government.

In January and February I attended several meetings with the Governor and his staff. But it was not until the morning of February 21, 1967, that I had a personal conversation with Reagan. We were attending a breakfast meeting at the Mansion Inn in Sacramento. The purpose of these early morning meetings was to forge a closer working relationship between Reagan and the Republican members of the legislature. On this particular morning I was one of eight Republican senators having breakfast with the Governor. As it turned out, I was seated next to him.

In the few minutes that we conversed I asked him some questions about various policy issues. In his response there was confident assurance. He was precise and specific about the things he intended to accomplish. I thought back to the speeches that I had heard him deliver during his campaign, and realized that he was now intensely determined to make the things he had talked about become reality. He was resolved to do everything in his power to reduce the size of government, to make it more accountable and more rational in all of its functions. If during all of those speeches no one else believed what he was preaching, there was no doubt that Ronald Reagan believed it, and was committed to make his vision reality.

I left the breakfast meeting wondering if he had any idea of the magnitude of the challenge before him, and frankly, doubting whether any man could mobilize the forces necessary to bring about the changes that Ronald Reagan envisioned. While I was pondering that thought Reagan had already unleashed one of the many initiatives that were to prove that he understood the magnitude of the challenge, and he had a plan on how he would deal with it.

Reagan conceived the idea of going to California's huge industrial and business base and asking for middle level executives to participate in a volunteer program to perform what he called "management audits" of the various agencies in state government. Reagan was confident that men and women from the private sector, who became known as Reagan's Raiders, could give a fresh look to the entire scope of state government and make recommendations that would be consistent with his commitment to the people of the state to "…cut, squeeze, and trim" the fat out of state government without diminishing the quality of the services provided to the people by the government.

From companies and professional firms all over the state hundreds of bright, well-educated men and women came forward to offer their time and talents, at no expense to the state. Under Reagan's direct sponsorship they were sent into every agency of the state government, to ask, to challenge, to examine, and to recommend.

They produced hundreds of pages of reports explaining how things could be done more effectively, for less cost.

Whenever possible Reagan would implement these recommendations by executive order. When legislative authority was required he would send his lieutenants to the senate and the assembly. He would ask the more visible and respected leaders of business and industry to assist him by making personal calls and visits to reluctant members of the legislature. It was a marvel to watch this tidal wave of power and public awareness sweep down upon the legislature. Reagan used these tactics on many occasions during his administration, with devastating effectiveness.

Gordon Luce was one of the men Reagan brought with him to Sacramento. Gordon first joined the Reagan administration as the state saving and loan commisioner and later became the Secretary of Business and Transportation. Over the years, as Luce's executive ability became more and more apparent he became one of the pivotal cabinet secretaries to the governor. On April 13, 1967, Gordon came to my office to discuss one of the changes suggested by some Reagan's Raiders who had gone through the executive agencies looking for ways to do things better for less cost. Gordon carefully explained the situation and the proposal and asked if the Governor could count on my support. I raised some questions about the proposal and asked Gordon to provide me with some answers.

Later in the day I was surprised to receive a telephone call from the Governor's office asking if I could meet with him and Gordon Luce. In the meeting I saw Reagan's determination to bring about the changes he had promised the electorate. I was a freshman state senator, the chronologically youngest member of the senate, and the least likely to have any influence over events in California for some time to come. Yet, there I was, sitting with the governor and Gordon Luce listening to the Governor answer the questions I had posed.

Reagan demonstrated that he understood the governmental processes that were involved, he understood the intent and the probable effect of the changes that he wanted made, and he understood that it would take the solid support of every Republican in the legislature (we were in the minority in both houses) in order to obtain his goal. This was not the aloof and uninformed "acting Governor" that the media so often ridiculed. This was a very determined chief executive who knew what he needed to accomplish and how to make it happen.

Soon however, Reagan was faced with a much more demanding challenge to his strength of character and his capacity as a leader, something much larger than the creation and implementation of an orderly approach to reducing the size and cost of state government. In America's universities across the nation, there was now a generation that had never known the sense of national commitment that prevailed during World War II. This generation had never been taught the ideals of service that had prevailed in the generation that had survived the 1930's, the period of the Great Depression. This new generation was about to explode in violent and irresponsible defiance of both the principles and the legacy that had guided and motivated prior generations.

Some thirty years later it is difficult to recreate in writing the sense of national angst that prevailed regarding the defiance of long accepted values that emerged between 1965 and 1975. The college-age generation had never known what it was like to sacrifice, and had no concept of what life was like in the depression and World War II. This new generation was abysmally ignorant of what it took to create employment for others, and decided they were going to give America instant justice for all and end the exploitation of the masses by the governing class. Not since the French revolution had there been as bizarre a period of turmoil and insanity created by largely ignorant militants as the United States experienced during the decade of 1965 to 1975.

The militants were primarily on America's college campuses. They were never able to mobilize more than a small fraction of the general student population, but a gullible and sympathetic news media combined with incompetent and cowardly university administrators allowed them to achieve power far beyond their numbers. The media, now increasingly dominated by the same leftist mentality, gave to the campus radicals acres of front page space and hours of television time. Like most radical causes, the rebels cloaked themselves in a mask of respectability. *Equality* and *democracy* were the buzz words meant to convey what they neither understood nor had any capacity to bring about.

Walter Berns is quoted by Dr. Victor Cline in his book entitled, *Where Do You Draw The Line?* in which Berns gives an illustration of how and why the campus turmoil of that decade was able to take place. He wrote:

> *Several years ago Cornell University paid $800 to a man to conduct (lead? Orchestrate? Create?) a 'happening' on campus as part of a festival of contemporary art. This happening consisted of the following: a group of students was led to the city dump where they selected the charred remains of an old automobile, spread it with several hundred pounds of strawberry jam, removed their shirts and blouses, and then danced around it, stopping occasionally to lick the jam. By 1970 standards this was not especially offensive; it was silly, as so many 'college boy' antics have been silly. What distinguishes it from goldfish swallowing and panty raids is that it was conducted under official university auspices and with the support of the administration and professors.*

The difference between Ronald Reagan and those who administered the college and university campuses in California during the decade of the late sixties and early seventies was that Reagan had the courage and the will to stand alone. He literally was alone in refusing to be intimidated by the radical and militant rabble. Up and down the state the faculties and administrators slunk away from confrontation with the rabble.

Judge Bill Clark cites this example from those days of campus turmoil. He said:

> *Very early in his first few months as Governor (1967) on a Saturday, with only a few hours notice served on the world, five thousand university of California faculty and students marched down the Mall (in Sacramento) with shrill speeches against the Governor, having heard an unsubstantiated report in the media that he was considering raising student tuition. Governor Reagan was scheduled to be with Governor McCall in Oregon the entire weekend. However, upon hearing of the proposed march, he canceled his Oregon trip to the dismay of his staff who felt he could have avoided the confrontation.*

> *The demonstrators marched down the mall and gathered in front of the Capitol building. Reagan remained in his office listening to the slanderous speeches, then quietly walked out of the capitol building and stood behind the speaker. The crowd of five thousand fell silent. Reagan took the microphone and immediately gained control of the day as he fearlessly and with absolute determination in his voice defended his past, present, and future conduct as the people's elected chief executive officer of the state. When he was finished some actually applauded, and the noisy rabble quietly wandered away.*

While the radical groups had their initial successes at midwestern universities, such as the University of Michigan, it was on the vast number of California university and college campuses where they found enough fellow travelers to try to bring down the entire institution. The campus administrators, mirroring the lack of conviction or commitment that frequently dominated most faculties, had no heart to withstand even the most feeble and harebrained assaults by the militants. Time after time the demonstrations and sit-ins would bring the entire university or college to its knees. Classes could not be held, faculty members dared not display any sense of outrage at what was going on, and hapless administrators would simply collapse and abandon any sense of commitment to maintaining the dignity and integrity of the institution.

In 1967, Ronald Reagan's first year as governor of California, the wildfire of campus turmoil was ready to explode into a total conflagration. In response to the student militants and their outrageous demands for ransom in the form of power and authority over the institution, Reagan had one message, which he expressed after the November 1966 election, but before he took office. The message to the militants was typical Reagan.

"Obey the *rules*, or get out." The rules prohibited destruction of state property, the disruption of class routine and curriculum, and public obscenities so typical in campus demonstrations.

Reagan's methods in dealing with the campus radicals gives clear insight into the character and the strength of the man. Had anyone of lesser commitment and strength of conviction been in the Governor's chair the results might have been far different. As Governor, he was the one who appointed the regents for the University of California and the trustees of the state university system. He also sat as a voting member of these bodies. In addition, he had the final word with regard to the huge appropriations out of the state treasury that financed the campuses. As direct and unequivocal as was his message to the militant students, Reagan's message to the faculty and administrators was equally direct and to the point. In effect he said, "If you can't run the place and keep order then I'll send someone in who can."

Clark Kerr, the President of the University of California, learned first hand what Ronald Reagan's wrath could mean. Kerr, used to being allowed to stand sanctimoniously on his pedestal of academic freedom, which in this instance meant academic license to chaos and capitulation, had his pedestal knocked out from under him in the first meeting of the University regents which Ronald Reagan attended. Reagan made it clear that he expected the administrators to bring order and dignity to the campus situation, to confront and suppress the radical militant activity, or to stand aside so he could deal with the situation directly. Early in Reagan's first few weeks as Governor the issue reached a climax, resulting in the university Board of Regents dismissing Kerr.

With his subsequent appointments to the board of regents and the trustees of the California state college system, Reagan made it clear he was not going to be intimidated by a sorry lot of self-appointed student reformers who in their entire lives had never produced anything of note except chaos and turmoil.

In September of 1967, at the San Jose State College campus, a militant student group decided that the presence of the Reserve Officer Training Corps (ROTC) on the campus was evidence of criminal war activities by the government. Accordingly, they began a campaign of harassment of the Air Force ROTC units that were marching on the athletic field. Reagan immediately contacted the chancellor of the state colleges, Glen Dumke, and made it clear he expected the campus president to take effective action or there would be some top to bottom changes made in the administration. The only action needed, and taken, was the suspension of the local leader of the radical SDS group who had instigated the disruption.

The above background lays the foundation for my several conversations with Reagan about the turmoil on the campuses and how to deal with it. During 1969 I visited every one of the University of California campuses, and six of the then state colleges. These visits included meetings with each of the college presidents, also faculty and students. As a result I prepared a package of legislation designed to deal with the turmoil and disruption taking place on the campuses.

On Tuesday, May 20, 1969, I had a lengthy meeting with Governor Reagan about this legislative package. He was supportive of the bills and wanted to add some amendments to them that he felt would help deal with some of the administrative problems made evident by the failure of campus presidents to deal with the radicals. In that meeting we talked at some length about our responsibilities as elected representatives of the tax paying public with regard to these increasingly destructive and frequently expensive demonstrations.

The Governor spent some time expressing his basic conviction to represent the people whose taxes were paying for the institutions of higher learning, whose children, for the most part, were neither involved in the disruptive conduct nor sympathetic with it. He was especially dismayed with the lack of courage and responsiveness from the administrators, both the system-wide officials and the individual campus presidents. Reagan felt that the people expected of him, and had a right to expect of him, the necessary leadership to protect their fundamental interests as taxpayers and as parents of students not involved in the chaotic undermining of the institution.

Reagan was convinced that a combination of liberal faculty and incompetent administrators made the riotous behavior possible. He shook his head with dismay at the feeble excuses that came back to him from the various administrators as to why they were unable to take decisive action in dealing with the disruptions. He found the contempt of the student militants for the rights of others incomprehensible.

"These are not fraternity panty raids," he said. "This is criminal conduct that has in it the seeds of bringing down the very core fabric of our society. If this group of hooligans is allowed to defy the law and the established order of society they could potentially bring down the entire nation."

This was a private conversation, not campaign rhetoric or political huckstering. Here was a man who felt keenly that the people had given to him the stewardship of protecting not only their tax dollars which pay for higher education but their constitutional heritage as well.

"I am not going to compromise my mandate by attempting to accommodate what these people are doing," he said. "I would rather lose the office and leave with my honor intact than live the rest of my life knowing that I failed to stand firm in the face of a challenge to my fundamental responsibility to the people."

I have often thought that Reagan's experience in dealing with the malcontents, the media who tried to protect and support them, and the liberals in the state legislature helped prepare him for the presidency. He never faltered in pursuing what he knew was the right course for himself as Governor. None of the above spheres of influence were able to sway him from his convictions or his decisions. In the end he triumphed over them all, and did so with the certainty of his convictions and the power of his resolve to pursue what he knew to be right.

I left his office aware that I had experienced a most remarkable moment of truth. He had allowed me to hear and feel the intensity of his most closely held convictions, and had done so with the assurance that our mutual commitment to those principles justified his candor in regard to the issues we discussed.

During1972 and 1973 there was a program on the Public Broadcasting Network called *The Advocates*. The program originated with WGBH, the PBS station in Boston. The format of the program was similar to courtroom procedure. The *trial* focused on a current topic of public interest, and then two advocates would act as the opposing attorneys. Each advocate had an opening and a closing statement, and two witnesses to support each side of the proposal that was on trial. Each advocate could cross examine the other's witnesses. During 1972 and 1973 I was one of the conservative advocates. Each show was an hour long.

My initial opponent in these debates was the former attorney general of Massachusetts, Michael Dukakis, later governor of the state and even later a Democratic candidate for president. Eventually Governor Dukakis moved to the position of judge on the program, in reality the moderator. The programs were taped once a month, primarily using the PBS studios in Boston, but sometimes Los Angeles.

At my request the producers of the show decided to do a program on the ballot initiative Reagan had sponsored, described in detail in chapter ten, a proposed amendment to the California state constitution which would limit the percentage of the gross personal income in the state that the legislature could tax. I was the advocate for the affirmative. For my two witnesses I selected Reagan and Nobel economist, Milton Friedman. The program was to be taped in Los Angeles. The taping was scheduled for the evening of Monday, October 29, 1973, at 9:00 p.m. The show was broadcast two days later. For each show a live audience was recruited by the host station.

On the day of the taping Reagan and I agreed to meet at his Los Angeles residence about 4:00 p.m. That would give us time to rehearse the points I wanted him to make as one of my two witnesses, and to prepare him for the cross examination by the other attorney. Earlier in the day I had met with my other witness, Dr. Friedman. After he and I had finished discussing his testimony in support of the

Reagan amendment, we spent some time discussing another topic which we both strongly supported, that of vouchers to be used by the parents of children from low income families in the public school system. Since I had been an active proponent of school vouchers in the California legislature it was a natural topic for the two of us to discuss. Dr. Friedman had written extensively in support of the school voucher concept.

When I met with Governor Reagan at his home I repeated to him a part of the conversation with Dr. Friedman. During the prior six years Reagan and I had had many conversations about education. I had functioned as the vice-chairman of the senate committee on education. In my book, *We Dare Not Fail*, I discussed at great length my own perception of many of the problems in public education, especially those challenges in the lower income communities.

As we discussed the reasons for using school vouchers to give parents the opportunity to put their children in better schools I learned more of Reagan's empathy for the economically disadvantaged. I also learned more of his antipathy for the monopolistic structure of public education and how, in his mind at least, it tended to stagnate if not actually erode all of the efforts the Governor and the legislature were making to improve the quality of public education. Here was a political leader who not only understood the philosophical issues involved, but was an ardent believer in applying the principles of the marketplace to public education.

Reagan expressed his frustration over the fact that it seemed as though anything we tried to do to upgrade the quality of public education would simply evaporate in the huge morass of the education establishment. With little more than a year remaining in his last term as governor, he still hoped to find the way to leave office with a public school system in the state that was more effective than the one in place when he took office.

Reagan said he wanted education to be the long term investment that would enable the children of the welfare recipient to escape from the bondage of the public dole. He strongly supported the school voucher concept because he was confident that many welfare parents, usually a mother functioning as a single parent, would eagerly grasp the opportunity to see their children participate in an educational structure where accountability and performance were rewarded. He expressed disgust with those who argued that a school voucher program would leave poor districts even poorer, and rich districts or private schools even richer.

We were in his living room. He was in his shirt sleeves with notepaper spread before him on the coffee table. He talked about education while in the middle of a working session on an entirely different subject. This was not a man talking to the audience or the camera, but expressing his own core values about what government owed the downtrodden, and the best way for government to give them the same opportunities and blessings of economic achievement that the rest of our society enjoyed. He wanted these people to be able to take their rightful place as successful contributing members of society. He wanted them to be able to give their children every possible opportunity to break out of the cycle of economic dependency. He also knew that to simply pour more money into the caldron of public education as it was then structured had little or no hope of producing the changes in the classroom that were so desperately needed.

That night, prior to the time when we were on camera, the Governor and Dr. Friedman discussed the school voucher issue. Reagan was as genuine and precise as he had been in the privacy of his own living room with me as his only listener. Milton Friedman was equally powerful in his analysis of the benefits the school vouchers would bring to pass. I introduced the producer of the program to the topic and he enthusiastically proposed that it should be the subject of another *Advocates* show.

I am amazed that nearly thirty years later, the debate is still going on. The debate over vouchers should have been over and settled long ago. It is a testimony to the power and the stultifying nature of the national and state teacher's unions that, notwithstanding the overwhelming evidence to the contrary, they are still able to oppose the school voucher concept as being *unfair* to the poor. Of course, the real basis for their success in opposing vouchers has been the financial commitment they make to the politicians of the Democratic Party, who in exchange for the money and the precinct working assistance of the school teachers, go on denying the poor children in America what would probably be the single most powerful tool for putting them on an equal educational footing with America's more affluent children.

On July 11, 1967, I was in the Governor's office for a meeting that involved more than just legislative issues, and so in addition to his two legislative liaisons, Jack Lindsey and Vern Sturgeon, other staff members were present as well. I was surprised to hear the conversation turn to the Republican nomination for president for the 1968 election. What really surprised me was the zeal with which the staff members began their analysis of why Ronald Reagan should seek that nomination. There was no doubt that this subject had been a matter of frequent discussion among the inner circle of Reagan's staff.

It was the first time I was involved in a discussion on the subject. Over the next ten years that conversation was to be repeated on many occasions in other forums. I don't know to what extent Reagan himself may have participated in such discussions. I have no doubt, however, that three years earlier, when he had campaigned so effectively for Barry Goldwater, the seed had been planted and the discussions in Sacramento would inevitably nurture that seed to full fruition.

A few weeks after this meeting Reagan demonstrated very decisively that he was not a shadow governor, letting others set his agenda and priorities. Two of Reagan's senior staff members who had been involved in the 1966 campaign and had come to Sacramento with him were found to be far more involved with the 1968 presidential maneuvering than Reagan had authorized. When the full extent of their conduct was made known to Reagan he was determined to slam the door on it immediately. He asked for the resignation of both gentlemen, sending a very clear message to the rest of the staff. He was captain of the ship, and intended to stay focused on being governor, not president, at least for the present. Reagan never again had to repeat that lesson while he was governor.

Notwithstanding Richard Nixon's California roots, in 1968 the California Republican Party made Governor Reagan their *favorite son* candidate for president, and the California delegation to the national convention was pledged to Reagan. Reagan left for the convention with the expectation that he would do whatever necessary for the best interests of the nation.

At the convention Reagan found a great deal of internal dissension among the conservative delegates. The so-called Rockefeller forces of the party were doing everything possible to besmirch the 1964 campaign of Senator Barry Goldwater. The incumbent vice president, Democrat Hubert Humphrey, had been seriously challenged by then Senator Robert Kennedy. A divided Republican Party could end up unwittingly aiding the ultimate election of Hubert Humphrey as president. The anti-Nixon contingency convinced Reagan and his advisors that a divided situation at the convention could lead to a Republican defeat in November. They persuaded Reagan and his advisors to launch a last minute attempt to win the nomination for Ronald Reagan.

I believe that Reagan never really thought he was running for president. He was attempting to find some way to heal the divisiveness within the Republican Party. Nonetheless, for two days Reagan attempted to obtain the nomination which Richard Nixon had already locked up during the previous four years by assisting obscure Republican candidates all over the country. Nixon had so many people committed to him long before 1968 came around that any thought of denying him the nomination was pointless.

Later I had the opportunity to raise that issue with Reagan. Why bother to enter the race for president when there seemed no possible way to succeed? He simply said: "We only listened to people who told us what we wanted to hear. They did not want Nixon. Yes, it was a mistake, but we learned a lot from it."

He had been used, and he knew it. There was no bitterness, just a quiet resolve to be wiser next time.

On Friday, July 19, 1968, the then Lt. Governor, Robert Finch, and I flew together from Burbank to Sacramento. Finch and I had attended a rally for Richard Nixon, for whom Finch had been chief of staff when Nixon was vice president to President Dwight Eisenhower. If Nixon could win the presidency in the coming November election, Finch would be going back to Washington as part of the Nixon administration. He talked candidly but quite perceptively of his relationship with Nixon and Reagan, and of his reaction to the Reagan phenomenon within the American political scene.

Finch was unwaveringly loyal to Nixon. Yet he had to admit that if Nixon only had Reagan's ability to deal with the media the public's perception of Nixon would be much more sympathetic, and in Finch's opinion, much more accurate. Finch then went on to describe his frustration over his inability to establish any after hours relationship with Reagan. Over the next several years I heard other people who worked closely with Reagan verbalize this same frustration, including Finch's successor as lieutenant governor, Ed Reinecke. As we flew to Sacramento, Finch talked about both Reagan and Nixon. He said:

"I have known Reagan for nearly two years, yet I am no closer to him now than the day we met. In our day to day working together he is gracious, deferential, and appropriately open and candid. But there is never any question that while we are close working associates we are not buddies, so to speak. If Reagan could only be as embracing in private as he is in public, and if Nixon could only be as embracing in public as he is in private, you would have the ultimate political leader."

Finch went on to describe how he and Richard Nixon would sit back, put their feet up on the coffee table, and have a free wheeling discussion about an issue, an individual, or some political tactic to be used with the congress or an opponent. "With Reagan," Finch complained, "you never had the sense that you had been given a place within the inner sanctum."

Ed Reinecke, who was appointed by Reagan to succeed Finch when Finch accepted a position in the Nixon cabinet, frequently voiced the same complaint. Reinecke and I had been close friends since 1962, and I was actively involved in his first campaign for Congress in 1964. His appointment as Lt. Governor was an example of Reagan's capacity to find and attract outstanding men to work with him. Reinecke had a clear future as a rising Republican star in Congress and an ultimate leader in the House of Representatives. Yet, when Reagan asked him to leave Congress to come to Sacramento as Lt. Governor, he willingly accepted the offer.

Reinecke was frustrated when he and his glamorous wife Jean tried to get the Reagan's to "…come out to the house for an evening so we can barbeque some steaks and visit." In my many conversations with Reinecke it became obvious that his biggest disappointment in his decision to come to Sacramento was the failure to establish that close personal bond with the Reagans. But for a railroaded conviction for perjury from a Washington, D.C. municipal court, Reinecke would have been Reagan's successor. Though the conviction was ultimately reversed by a court of appeals Reinecke never recovered his political base. Neither did he ever enter into the "inner sanctum" of Ronald Reagan's personal life.

My purpose in sharing these anecdotes has to do with my own perception of Reagan's sense of mission in his political career. Reagan's rapport with those individuals who were associated with him on a daily basis was ever one of purpose. He made certain those individuals were encouraged and motivated to provide him the most effective support and professional competence possible. In the truest sense of masterful leadership and administrative effectiveness he had the capacity to bring out the best in the people around him. He had the capacity to make them feel that he was depending on them in a very personal sense. No one wanted to run the risk of incurring his disappointment if they failed to perform up to his expectations.

People who worked closely with Reagan's two most honored predecessors as president, George Washington and Abraham Lincoln, expressed this same frustration that Bob Finch, Ed Reinecke, and others experienced with Reagan. The truth is that all three of these presidents essentially looked within for the emotional, intellectual, and spiritual strength to pursue their objectives. Washington was a loner in leading the military campaigns of the Revolutionary War, and later in his two terms as president of an infant nation. Lincoln's determination to save the Union and bring the nation out of the agony of the Civil War, and Ronald Reagan's determination to end the Cold War with the Soviet Union all required a leader whose inner strength and clarity of purpose would not yield to disappointment or momentary setback. All three men were essentially "loners" because there was no one near whose single-minded determination equaled their own.

But for Reagan, there were very few to whom he could turn to for rejuvenation of intellectual, emotional, and spiritual power. Even when he socialized with friends, playing cards or discussing events of the day, there were seldom personal moments. The only people that I felt ever had this special place in his life were his wife, Nancy, his brother, Neil, and Bill Clark.

Very few people seem to have recognized the depth of the relationship between Bill Clark and Reagan. The essence of that relationship was expressed by Edmund Morris, the man selected to be the official biographer of Ronald Reagan. In the November/December 1999 issue of *The American Enterprise (TAE)* magazine, Morris gave an interview in which he quite perceptively analyzed the unique relationship between the two men. The interview went as follows:

> *TAE: Was there a particular advisor in Reagan's inner circle who was the most impressive?*
> *Edmund Morris: Oh, yes, Bill Clark.*
> *TAE: Judge Clark, as he was known. He was Reagan's chief of staff as governor, and later in Washington he was his National Security Adviser and Secretary of the Interior.*
> *Morris: Clark was so private, quiet, and unflamboyant that he's now largely forgotten. But he's the most important and influential person in the first (Reagan) administration, and in fact, the only person in the entire two terms who had any kind of spiritual intimacy with the President.*

Both as governor in Sacramento and as president in Washington,

D.C., Reagan would follow much the same pattern in dealing with a difficult problem. If it had some elements of being a legal problem he would call William French Smith, who served him faithfully as a private attorney outside of government in California, and as his first attorney general in Washington. If it were a personnel problem, he would go over it with Ed Meese, the chief of staff when Reagan was governor and counselor to the president in the White House.

When the issue with which Reagan was dealing had moral overtones, an issue such as abortion or various facets of education or welfare reform, Reagan would turn to Bill Clark. A devout Roman Catholic, and a man of exceptional personal integrity and dignity, Clark's quiet demeanor and lack of desire for personal aggrandizement belied the depth and strength that Reagan recognized within him. When it was important to Ronald Reagan to search for the spiritual soul of an issue, it was to Bill Clark that he turned.

As governor Reagan seldom turned to people outside of his official circle. If, after discussing a matter with Ed Meese and the rest of his staff, he still needed to get some further input, he would turn to Holmes Tuttle or others in his "kitchen cabinet." It was also common knowledge among those who worked with him in Sacramento and Washington that he placed great reliance upon Nancy and her counsel.

It would be both presumptuous and impossible for me to make any valid analysis of the unity and rapport between Ronald Reagan and his wife, Nancy. Ed Meese, who saw the two of them perhaps as much as anyone, noted it this way:

"He did depend on Nancy—it was a bad day for him if she was not there when he got home. He was not comfortable in being home without her. On the other hand, when we went on trips and she was not there he was always very affable with the staff—he was always very gracious. But there was never any doubt that Nancy was his most trusted advisor and source of strength and assurance."

I can never remember a time when Ronald Reagan seemed depressed or emotionally down. I never remember a time when his mood was unpleasant, aloof or removed. This was part of the inner strength that was so much a part of his nature. It is also a very real part of the answer to why he was in many ways a man who stood alone. Ronald Reagan did not lean on others when he needed extra strength. In another chapter I describe some of our conversations about prayer. He did pray, and he found strength and assurance in prayer. When he needed another reservoir of strength outside of his own intellect and spirit, it was in Nancy Reagan or in his clasped hands, fingers pointing upward in prayer.

I asked Ed Meese to describe Reagan during times of severe stress. Ed's insightful description says it all:

"There were times when he was filled with great concern, such as during the Iran-Contra affair. I could see that he was feeling the tension. At the beginning when the media and the liberal columnists were gleefully anticipating that they had another president in the midst of a Watergate scandal, I said to him: 'Mr. President, I hope this whole thing isn't getting you down.' He smiled and said, 'No Ed, I don't have to worry—Nancy worries enough for both of us'."

The answer was a well deserved tribute to Nancy. It was also descriptive of his own ability to suffer and perhaps bleed internally, but still carry on with every outward expression of confident assurance that in the end he would prevail.

In chapter one I quoted from a speech given by Reagan in the fall of 1962 that included some comments about the Cold War. Eighteen years before becoming president, Ronald Reagan already had a clear vision of what he wanted to do about the Cold War. Some years later he became a part of the Peace Through Strength Coalition. This was still many years prior to his becoming president. He felt that the U.S.

had to be strong enough militarily to be able to engage the Soviets. He believed with all his heart that communism was morally wrong and that we should not shrink from that view. Hence, the "Evil Empire" speech.

In response to my question as to whether or not Reagan had entered the White House with a clear vision of how he would deal with the Cold War, Ed Meese said:

"I am not certain he had a specific vision of destroying the Soviet Union—but he recognized that the Soviets were desperately short of cash in their economy, and that they could not afford to keep up with the United States in a military buildup. He recognized that he could use the immense wealth of the U.S. government to ultimately push the Soviets into a position of meaningful negotiation."

In chapter eleven I deal more specifically with the issue of how Ronald Reagan was a man who literally changed the world. He did this through the economic policies that became known as Reaganomics, and his literal defeat of the Soviet Union by winning the Cold War. Reagan had long pondered the state of a world in which two super powers toyed with mutual annihilation as an essential element of their foreign policy. The vision of what must be done to restore a sense of peace and security in the world became firmly established in Reagan's mind prior to assuming the presidency.

I have previously mentioned that when President Richard Nixon returned from his initially secret trip to China he sent Henry Kissinger to California to brief Governor Ronald Reagan about the decision to establish diplomatic relations with China. Kissinger flew into Sacramento in the late afternoon, and he and Governor Reagan met at the Governor's residence. It so happened that the next morning I was in a meeting with the Governor when he described the conversation with Kissinger. The point of this story is that Reagan concluded his summary of the meeting with this remarkably prophetic comment:

"If I am ever the President, I can guarantee that the Secretary of State will have no doubt in his mind who is Secretary of State and who is President."

Soon after beginning his first term as president, Reagan was faced with a particularly difficult challenge that ultimately demonstrated his strength as a leader and that he was a man who could, when necessary, stand alone. There were strong differences of opinion among Reagan's key foreign policy advisors. At the same time that he was dealing with this issue someone discovered an envelope that held ten thousand dollars in cash in the private office safe of the National Security Advisor, Richard Allen. The media was having a field day. Reagan was trying to figure out how to handle all of this. Replacing Dick Allen with Judge William Clark seemed like a way to settle things down. Clark came over from the state department, but that did not settle things. Haig was pressing his claim to have sole authority over foreign affairs by threatening to resign. In fact he resigned several times, and each time Reagan talked him out of it.

The situation with the foreign policy advisors remained in a state of turmoil. Haig was continually complaining that neither Casey nor Weinberger had any business being involved in foreign policy. Reagan's style was to listen to all his advisors. He liked to get a variety of opinions on critical issues before he made a decision. Haig never seemed to understand that.

On the third time that Haig threatened to resign because others were being allowed to meddle in his domain, Reagan said: "Okay, Al, if that is the way you feel about it, then I have no choice but to accept your resignation…" That is when George Schulz came in as the new secretary of state. Even though Reagan did not want to lose the services of Al Haig, and did not want to give the media the chance to capitalize on the apparent state of discord in the cabinet, when the situation could no longer be tolerated Reagan did what needed to be done. He was a man of action, and when action was needed, it took place with what became known in Washington as "Reagan's terrible swift sword."

In his comments to the American people immediately after he took the oath of office as President of the United States, Gerald Ford demonstrated the difference between himself and Ronald Reagan as a leader. Henry Kissinger had been Nixon's Secretary of State. Whatever else Gerald Ford may have said in his brief speech has long been forgotten. But, to assure the American people that he would not have to stand alone, President Ford said: "…I am happy to inform you that Henry Kissinger has confirmed that he will remain as the Secretary of State."

Ronald Reagan did not need to have anyone standing by his side, particularly if that individual was confused about who was the leader in charge. He could and often did stand alone.

There is an indescribable degree of pathos in the fact that near the end of his mortal life Ronald Reagan literally became a man alone. His suffering with Alzheimer's disease took away the ability of the world to reach him, and for him to reach the world. There was so much we could learn from him after he was no longer in public office. Given the desecration of the Oval Office by one of his successors, it is likely a blessing that the disease had taken from him the need to suffer pain and sorrow at what had transpired in a place he regarded as a sacred shrine. In the Oval Office Ronald Reagan seldom even removed his suit coat, so deeply did he reverence the legacy of that room, particularly in those times when as the leader of the free world he was *a man who stood alone.*

SEVEN
WISDOM & HUMOR

Early in his first term Governor Reagan and I had a very stormy confrontation that in retrospect illustrated both his wisdom and his self control. On Thursday, March30, 1967, I met with him twice. The first meeting included Republican legislators whom the Governor wanted to hear a proposal from assemblyman John Veneman, a proposal which the Governor had agreed to support to deal with the financial problems of Medi-Cal.

In the meeting I expressed strong opposition to the proposal and said I could not support it. Veneman, who later went to Washington with the Nixon Administration in the Department of Health and Welfare, had structured a refinancing arrangement for Medi-Cal that gave more power to the federal government, weakening the ability of the state legislature to modify the Medi-Cal program in the future.

Later in the day I was invited to meet again with the Governor, this time in a one on one meeting. He listened carefully to my reasons for opposing the Veneman plan. Basically I was opposed to further encroachment by the federal government, particularly in the areas of health and welfare programs.

Reagan said he was in total harmony with my rationale, but he was facing a financial crisis over the state's obligations to the Medi-Cal program. He had been told he had to make fundamental changes to the financing and administrative structure of Medi-Cal or the state's cost burden would go far beyond the ability to pay. Reagan was absolutely determined not to be forced to ask for a tax increase.

At that point the conversation became heated. My zeal to stand on principle was somewhat intemperate, and Reagan seemed offended by my presumptuousness and insensitivity. I told him that in my opinion he was failing to stand by his convictions. He was succumbing to the pressures from the liberals to compromise the campaign promises he had made only a year earlier.

I had heard about Ronald Reagan's fierce Irish temper. But the thing I learned that day was that he was master of his emotions. I confess the statements I made in the intensity of the discussion were intemperate and brash, but he kept his composure even while the blood vessels in his neck were bulging with the pressure caused by his rising fury. Finally he made a proposal that illustrated his skill as a negotiator and his adeptness in dealing with the realities that confronted him, notwithstanding his apparent desire to follow a different path.

"Look," he said, "I am just as dedicated to resisting further federal encroachment upon the states rights as you are. I've been sitting in this chair for ninety days and now have to solve a huge problem that I did not create. Can you put on my desk right now a proposal to restructure this mess, a proposal that will have the support of all the Republicans and enough Democrats to pass as an emergency statute? Because if you can, I'll sign it."

I could not deliver any such proposal, and told him so. Assemblyman Veneman and his liberal sidekicks on the Republican side of the assembly had been involved in creating the mess, and they were now in a position to force Reagan to go along with them or be labeled early in his administration as incapable of effectively resolving the first major challenge to his leadership. Reagan recognized the dynamics of the situation, and though it violated his personal political philosophy, he had to deal with reality. Now he had to step aside or see his credibility as governor evaporate, at least in part.

Having maneuvered me into a corner, he used the Reagan charm and leadership skills to save my dignity while bringing me closer into his sphere of influence. He said:

"If you will work with me now, I'll work with you later to find a better way to do this. You have my word that when we create a solution to this problem more consistent with what we believe, it will have my total support."

I accepted his commitment and the meeting ended. As I think back on that experience, I appreciate more than ever his skill as a leader. I was a freshman senator, but he knew in the future he would need my support. Instead of reacting as many might have done to the intemperate and disrespectful way in which I responded to his dilemma, he kept his composure and effectively recruited my allegiance for this and future legislative battles.

Reagan's challenge to "find a better way" remained in my mind. I went back to my office, assembled my staff, and told them we were going to research this issue and come back to the Governor with solutions. I expected those solutions would be in the form of legislative proposals, and during the next several years many of them were presented to the Governor and he supported them.

One additional result of Reagan's challenge to "...find a better way" was that the research my staff and I did on this and other issues became the basis for a book which we called *We Dare Not Fail*. Subsequent to this conversation with Reagan there were other less confrontational conversations dealing with public education, welfare reform, and a variety of similar issues that needed to be resolved. All of these issues presented similar challenges, reconciling political philosophy and the application of conservative principles of government to the practical matter of solving real world problems. The research on these issues provided the basis for the book.

In January, 1968, I presented to Reagan the first copy of the book, *We Dare Not Fail.* A few days later he called me to say that he liked the book enough that he wanted every member of his cabinet to read it. I asked him if I could quote him, and he said, "Absolutely." Accordingly, we called the printer and printed a hundred thousand paste-on tags, one for the front of each copy of the book which read,

Must Reading for My Cabinet—Ronald Reagan.

Several weeks later, a senior Democrat in the senate, who was chairman of the senate finance committee, told me about a conversation with Reagan. The senator had been in the Governor's office discussing some budget issues that would pass through his committee. I had given him a complimentary copy of the book, with Reagan's endorsement on the cover. In a relaxed moment with Reagan he asked the Governor if he was aware that his endorsement was on the front of my book and that it was must reading for the Governor's senior appointees. It would have been easy for Reagan to simply smile and say that his endorsement was a matter of necessity rather than conviction. Instead, according to my democratic colleague, Reagan said:

"Yes, and I mean it. Harmer's approach to many of these issues is absolutely on target and I hope to see you guys up there (the Senate Chamber was two floors above the governor's offices) enacting some bills to carry out his ideas."

The chairman of the senate finance committee was an old political manipulator. He had been around Sacramento for a number of years and was familiar with the games that had to be played in order to achieve an end result. It was common practice inside the capitol to tell three different people three different things about the same issue, if that is what it took to get their support. He candidly admitted to me that he was surprised at Reagan's response, and somewhat perplexed by his adamant defense of the content of the book.

I learned two things about Ronald Reagan at a buffet dinner at his home on the evening of Monday, March 6, 1967. The first of those lessons had to do with his intellectual capacity. He demonstrated his ability to carry on a very substantive conversation while at the same time remaining totally aware of a television camera crew that had entered the room. Without any interruption in his chain of thought or any apparent distraction of his attention from those to whom he was speaking he was continually aware of the location and conduct of the camera crew. As the camera crew moved about the room, Reagan was very casually adjusting his position so that he was always on camera. I realized that his mind was capable of dealing with two entirely separate issues at the same time.

The second thing I observed that evening was his ability to listen to a proposal that was never going to be acceptable to him. While being careful not to compromise his opposition to the concept involved, he also refrained from offending or alienating the proponent. One of the senior Democrats in the state senate approached the governor and raised the issue about Reagan's opposition to a legislative proposal that senator was sponsoring Reagan listened to the senator's argument for the rapid enactment and approval of the proposal. The man was determined to keep the Governor from making any retreat until he defended his presentation.

Reagan smiled, with a facial gesture that seemed to convey the assurance that here was a friend trying to give some advice in a kindly manner.

"Well, let me tell you how I expect to deal with that," he said, and then told a story that was both humorous and yet illustrated the point he wanted to make. But the lesson I learned that night and saw repeated endlessly throughout the next eight years was the tactic of using a story to avoid having to tell people that he already knew what he wanted to do about an issue – and it was not what they had in mind.

Reagan then graciously excused himself to go talk with other guests, and my democratic colleague turned to the three of us still remaining, all Republicans. I asked him what he thought the Governor would do with this bill if it ever reached his desk.

"You just heard him say that he likes the idea," he said.

I hadn't heard any such thing—but I did hear a master of human understanding defuse a potential confrontation with so much warmth and assurance, and a total lack of acrimony, that it was impossible to take offense.

On many occasions after that night I saw Reagan exercise that same ability to listen graciously and attentively to a presentation with which he was in total disagreement without alienating the individual making the presentation. Reagan's mind seemed to operate on two wave lengths at the same time. In the micro sense, he was attentive to and responsive to the person or persons with whom he was speaking. At the same time, in the macro sense, he always seemed aware of the broader picture. It didn't matter if he was in a crowded office, his dining room at home, or in a huge banquet hall, he remained in constant contact with the dynamics of everything going on about him while he listened to and responded to the individual or individuals with whom he was speaking. There were usually others present who were passive participants in the conversation. He was acutely sensitive to that fact and effectively controlled the situation in both the macro and micro sense.

In his dealing with those about him, Reagan demonstrated a remarkable degree of wisdom. Ed Meese put it this way:

"He treated all of the staff with deference—to him they were all entitled to the respect of their service and status. He did not see people in categories of importance—he regarded them all as pretty much alike."

In Sacramento Ed Meese, Helene Von Damm, Bill Clark, Michael Deaver, and Lyn Nofziger were the staff people closest to him. Dr. Alex Sheriffs, Reagan's principal staff person for education, seemed to have a particularly close relationship with Reagan—partly because they were closer in age. On various occasions I have heard each one of these former staff members describe a situation in which the Governor exhibited both wisdom and humor in a manner that enabled him to confirm and enhance the loyalty of a staff person or member of the legislature.

On one occasion when I was meeting with Reagan in my capacity as the caucus chairman for the Republicans in the state senate, the issue arose of who in the senate we might ask to be the author of a very sensitive and important piece of legislation. Several names were mentioned, and the Governor's staff and I proposed an individual that we thought could be relied upon to successfully fulfill the mission. Reagan listened to my recommendation and then responded with a story.

It is difficult to recapture in writing Reagan's ability to use humor because the written word cannot replicate Reagan's delightful ability to mimic accents. In this case, the accent was an Illinois farmer of the mid 1850's. Reagan often would refer to Abraham Lincoln's use of humor and in this instance he borrowed a story that Lincoln used when he was asked to defend why he continued to keep General McClellan as commander of the Army of the Potomac during the Civil War. The story went something like this:

> There was a farmer in downstate Illinois who had some fighting cocks. One of them was notorious for never being willing to actually fight. Time and time again when actually put into the cockpit with another bird, even one much smaller than himself, the

farmer's cock would turn and run. Finally an exasperated friend who had bet on the farmer's bird and lost his wager demanded to know why he continued to keep that bird in the fighting camp. The old farmer hung his head for a moment and then looking up he responded:

"Waal, I know that in a fight he ain't worth a soggy corn cob, but he sure is hell on parade."

I got the message and we finally agreed on another individual. As events unfolded it became evident that in this particular situation Reagan's ability to assess an individual's strengths and weaknesses was totally accurate. His perception of the man whom he declined to recruit to introduce the legislation, and the individual that we did recruit who performed exactly as Governor Reagan predicted he would, was remarkable.

The same is certainly true with regard to those individuals that Ronald Reagan brought into the senior levels of California state government. Far from being the former B movie actor who was way over his head, as the press delighted in describing him, Ronald Reagan was an executive of consummate skill in assessing the capability of those whom he selected to work with him. That skill demonstrated not only the quality of his leadership, but it was a manifestation of very remarkable wisdom and intellect.

Another aspect of Ronald Reagan's wisdom was his decision-making process. I learned early that Governor Reagan did not like to be pressed for a decision until he had been able to "...round table this with the fellows." He wanted all those involved to have the opportunity to be heard. It was important to him to maintain faith with the people who had agreed to work in the trenches beside him. Usually he did not make decisions on critical matters until he was certain he had the support and concurrence of those who would have to carry out the decision.

Ed Meese observed these same qualities in the way Reagan as President dealt with his cabinet members and foreign leaders. In the prior chapter I recited how in his first term the Secretary of State, Alexander Haig, began complaining about how Casper Weinberger, the Secretary of Defense, and CIA Director Casey continued delving into matters that Haig felt were the exclusive responsibility of the State Department.

"The State Department insisted on running everything," Meese said. "Reagan's style was to round table a matter with his closest advisors and staff members, irrespective of whether or not it was directly within their sphere of responsibility. He wanted to hear everyone's views. Cap Weinberger, who had served with Reagan in California, understood the President's desire to hear other views. Cap could be very strong willed but knew how Reagan wanted to function."

"Secretary Haig, on the other hand, could never seem to understand Reagan's desire to obtain the counsel and insight of those about him."

The fact that Secretary Haig could never accommodate himself to this style of leadership finally became the factor that made it necessary for Reagan to let him resign from the cabinet.

In his first term as president, Reagan resisted the pressure from many so-called experts in foreign policy to meet with the Soviet leadership. From the time that he first took office he was urged by the media and Congress to enter into direct negotiations with Soviet leaders. In an almost bizarre sequence of events, three successive Soviet leaders, Breznev, Andropov, and Chernenko, all died in office during the first four years after Reagan became President. His first meeting with a Soviet leader was in November, 1985, when he and Mikhail Gorbachev met at Geneva.

That meeting was tightly structured with staff and senior officials and translators in the same room with the two principals. Reagan knew that he could never really get through to Gorbachev in this setting. On his own, Reagan discovered that down near the lake was a rustic cabin, not large enough for the formal meetings, but with a fireplace and decor that were ideal for a more intimate exchange of views.

During the formal meeting Reagan suggested that the two men go for a walk down by the lake. When they reached the cabin Reagan invited Gorbachev to come in, and with only the interpreters present, they sat down for a much more informal and intimate discussion. Ed Meese describes the situation this way:

"When he first took office he didn't want to meet with a Soviet leader until he had been able to strengthen the military so he could negotiate from a position of strength. Then he wanted to assure the Soviet leader that the U.S. was not a threat to them, that the U.S. meant no harm to the Soviet Union. That is exactly what he did when he took Gorbachev off alone for a private chat. The President was very much committed to the concept later verbalized by Texas senator Phil Gramm, '...when the time comes for the lion to lie down with the lamb, I want to be sure that the United States is the lion.' This is why Reagan worked so hard to strengthen the military."

The results of that private informal chat are now history. A man of great wisdom laid the foundation for bringing to pass the most significant foreign policy accomplishment since the end of World War II, the dissolution of the Soviet Union, and with it, the end of the Cold War.

Even in Sacramento Reagan voiced strong convictions about the danger of communism. He knew first hand how the communists had attempted to infiltrate the motion picture industry. Beginning in the early 40's he studied communism and the communist mentality. It was this study and experience that created his intense opposition to that ideology and system of government.

Ed Meese explained how Reagan, as president, dramatically

changed the official government thinking on how to deal with the communists.

"He did not regard detente as a valid policy for opposing Communism. Detente was the mode of the sixties and seventies—but in the Reagan presidency detente was never allowed to become a part of the president's thinking.

"He was not belligerent or provocative, but he was very honest and straightforward with the Soviets and with the rest of the world. He wanted the Soviets to know how he looked upon their activity and their philosophy, and he wanted the rest of the world to have a clear understanding of how he regarded the communist philosophy."

In his speeches to the British parliament in 1982 and to the Christian Coalition in 1983 President Reagan gave voice to his determination to eliminate the threat of communist domination in any part of the world, including the nations then under the communist yoke. Many of his advisors urged him not to be so precise about the evils of communism, and the liberal media was totally predictable in ranting that Ronald Reagan's approach to dealing with the communists would lead us into the third world war.

Ed Meese noted that the one thing President Reagan wanted the staff and the cabinet to understand was that they should be prepared to comment openly and candidly. He needed and wanted to hear all sides of an issue.

In the prior chapter I referred to the situation involving the National Security Advisor, Richard "Dick" Allen that could have been extremely damaging to Reagan.

When the media broke this story their bias was to make their audience assume that the situation was supposedly filled with scandal. An envelope with Japanese writing on it was found in Dick Allen's office safe, with ten thousand dollars in cash in it. The media began to immediately trumpet the story with implications that Allen had taken the money for himself, some kind of bribe.

Reagan could have involved himself in the situation and attempted to defuse the media spotlight. Instead, he called in Ed Meese, the White House counselor to the President, and William French Smith, the attorney general and the nation's chief law enforcement officer. Reagan's instructions to them were quite clear and unequivocal.

"Find out what is at the bottom of this," he said, "and then let's do whatever has to be done to rectify the situation."

When Meese and Smith were through investigating the matter, it was clear that Allen was not really in a compromised situation. The money that Allen had placed in his safe had been presented to Mrs. Reagan as a gift from a Japanese delegation that had come to meet the president. For the Japanese this was a customary means of showing respect. When Allen saw what was happening he graciously took the envelope for Mrs. Reagan. He had simply put the money in his safe and then forgotten about it.

Even though he was personally exonerated, the publicity had become so widespread, and the media slanting of the story against Allen so negative, that he voluntarily opted to resign rather than put the President through the discomfort of having to continue to explain away the conduct of both his Japanese guests and the National Security Advisor. Richard Allen's resignation opened the way for the appointment of William Clark as the president's national security advisor. Clark at that time was the deputy secretary of state. In Bill Clark Reagan had a tested, trusted, former chief of staff. Clark was not only a very capable administrator and counselor, he was also very close to the president in their personal relationship. As national security advisor Clark not only provided Reagan with competent analysis of communist aggression throughout the world, but he also provided counsel and support on a variety of other issues.

Another significant dimension of Ronald Reagan's decision making process was his refusal to allow partisan political considerations to influence policy issues. He was not willing to compromise his integrity by allowing the question of what would be best for his personal political benefit or that of the Republican party. Very early in his first term as governor we all learned that questions of policy were to be determined on the basis of merit and not political consideration.

Perhaps the most overlooked evidence of the wisdom of Ronald Reagan was his sense of humor. The media would have the world believe that Ronald Reagan had no capacity to deal with the complicated and profoundly demanding issues facing the President, so he spent his time telling jokes. Nothing could be farther from the truth. Reagan's sense of humor and his finely tuned ability to tell stories had very practical and vital purposes.

First of all, to make certain that things remained in perspective he laughed at himself. It kept him from getting depressed over the immense challenges he was facing. Most of the time his humor was self-deprecating. His Irish jokes were really jokes on himself. Once in the midst of a tremendous battle with his opposition in the Congress, as Reagan and his staff were attempting to craft a strategy that would make it possible to obtain their objective, Reagan looked at Ed Meese, and with that twinkle in his eye said, "Well, Ed, we Irish have a marvelous quality that has saved us from defeat over the centuries—malice!"

He then laughed at himself and returned to the issue of deliberating how to deal with his congressional opponents.

Abraham Lincoln often used humor to illustrate the issue at hand and the principle he was advocating. Lincoln used humor in his debates with political opponents, as a means of answering their arguments and emphasizing his own closeness to the common man.

Lincoln's stories and humor included words and situations to which the average farmer in Illinois could readily relate.

Reagan borrowed much of Lincoln's humor and used humor in the same way that Lincoln did. With his marvelous ability to mimic the Irish accent much of the humor was a means of laughing at himself. Following is an example.

"There was a certain priest named Patrick sent down from Ireland to a parish near London. Unfortunately this priest was an especially ardent Irishman, and among other things was very anti-English. He consistently had to be called in by the bishop and reprimanded for his denigrating of the English from the pulpit.

"Finally the bishop called him in and told him that this was his last chance. Said the bishop, 'Father Patrick, if you give one more sermon in which you offend the English members of the parish then you will have to be transferred to some remote parish outside of the British kingdom.'

"Quite contrite, Father Patrick promised that he would obey the bishop's instructions.

"The next Sunday was Palm Sunday, the Sunday prior to Easter. As he was reciting the events during the Last Supper, Father Patrick paraphrased the words of Christ as he said in a very heavy Irish brogue, 'Sure lads, and it breaks me heart to know that one of you will betray me.' To which Judas stood up and replied, (in a very distinctive English accent)'Blimey Governor, do you suppose it could be me.'"

On those occasions when he might need to engage in some partisan humor, Reagan had a story about another minister of the gospel. The locale for this story was in Mississippi, and again, Reagan's ability to mimic an accent was used to perfection. The story went as follows:

"This story takes place just at the turn of the century. A young minister has just graduated from the theological seminary, and his first assignment is in rural Mississippi. When he gets off the train he finds that the hour is late in the day, and the train station is about twelve miles from his destination. Not knowing what else to do he starts to walk down the dusty country road toward the little town where his flock awaits him. As the sun gets lower in the heaven he remembers having heard of the large variety of snakes that inhabit this area.

"However, a local farmer comes along in a wagon and offers him a ride. He gratefully accepts and after they have journeyed just a short distance the farmer asks, 'What are your politics?'

"'Why I'm a Republican,' says the young minister.

"The farmer stops and wagon and tells him to get out. Confused the young minister asks what he did to offend his benefactor. The farmer simply replies, 'Haint never been a Republican ride in this wagon and I'm not going to risk lettin one talk me into changin my politics now.'

"So the young minister gets out and is walking along the dusty road.

"After some time another wagon comes along. The driver offers him a ride which he gratefully accepts. In a few minutes the question is again posed, 'What are your politics?' Looking at the setting sun, and the suspicious creatures that his eyes picked out by the side of the road, he paused and then responded, 'I'm a Democrat.'

"They rode on a short distance when the driver stopped beside a field of watermelons. He asked the young minister to help him load some of them into the wagon.

"'Is this your farm?' the minister asked.

"'No,' replied the wagoneer, 'but he ain't goin to miss these. Just hep me put in a dozen or so.'

"The young minister protested. 'I can't do a thing like that—I'm a minister of the gospel.'

"The wagon driver got right to the point. 'You're still six miles away from town, it's almost dark, and ain't no one else likely to come this way tonight. You can hep me load some mellons, or you can start walkin.'

"The young minister looked at the setting sun, the dusty road, and finally agreed to help. "As he was on his knees gathering a melon he looked heavenward, and then prayed:

"'Oh Lord, forgive me. I've been a Democrat for ten minutes and already I'm a thief.'"

Ronald Reagan's ever cheerful personality made it easy to listen to his humor. Pleasant as it was, the Reagan repertoire of jokes and stories had a more vital purpose than entertainment. It was his most effective weapon to get an opponent to hear Reagan's side of the story. Also, it was a way to remind himself and his critics that we are all only mortal.

EIGHT

FAITH & CHARITY

Each January in Sacramento, at the California State Capitol, the governor sponsored a non-denominational prayer breakfast. In attendance were members of the legislature, the various government officials and bureaucrats who were in Sacramento, the Governor and his principal staff. There were usually three speakers, one of whom represented the legislature. In 1972 I was asked to be the representative of the legislature. I chose to speak to the topic, *What My Faith Means to Me.* The essential thrust of my talk was to show how genuine faith in God gives the believer a sustaining power to handle disappointment, frustration, confusion, and uncertainty. I said prayer was the essential expression of real faith in God. From prayer came the faith to deal with the vicissitudes of life.

After the breakfast I received a telephone call from Reagan. He thanked me for the talk and then we spent about ten minutes discussing the importance of prayer in our own lives. He was not attempting to court my favor or good will, or to somehow assure me that he too was a believer in prayer. Rather, he seemed to just want to talk with someone who shared his views about faith in prayer, and praying in faith. As I listened to his comments I concluded that he was hungry for the opportunity to be comfortable in describing to others what his own faith in God, and in prayer, meant to him.

That telephone conversation established a new level of personal rapport between us that on various future occasions enabled us to talk, usually only briefly, about the benefits of prayer in our personal lives. It also opened the door to other conversations and experiences that allowed me to see, ever so briefly, the fundamental values of his religious convictions. I came to understand and know that Ronald Reagan had a very deep and abiding faith in the existence of God, in the power and blessing of prayer, and a sustaining conviction that his prayers were heard and that the events of his life were continually blessed by the power of the Supreme Being.

Later that year, on Tuesday, September 21, we spent much of the day working together on some negotiations with the Democratic leaders from the legislature. We finished at about 4:30, and shortly thereafter left for the airport to fly down to Los Angeles in a Cessna Citation that the state had leased. As I recall, we landed at the Santa Monica airport. From there we went to the home of Richard Gulbranson, in the area of North Hollywood known as Toluca Lake. The event was a dinner to raise funds for the Republican candidate in the 48th assembly district. Richard Gulbranson was the Los Angeles County Republican chairman. Reagan and I left the Gulbranson residence at about 9:30 p.m. and drove back to the airport.

Since we had spent much of the day together, and it had been a very intense day, I assumed he would want to rest during the flight back to Sacramento. I just closed my eyes and leaned back to try to get some sleep. No sooner had I done so than he was squeezing my elbow.

"I want to ask you a question," he said. "What do you think is the most important announcement that could be made to all the world?"

The question sounded suspiciously similar to what a Mormon missionary might ask. Given Reagan's penchant for joking I was halfway suspicious that he was pulling my leg. But as I looked at him I could tell he was quite serious and the question very genuine. So, I decided to be very genuine in my response.

"The return of Jesus Christ," I said.

"Exactly," Reagan responded. "Let's talk about it."

Instead of resting from the fatigue of that very long day he was anxious to get into a rather deep and intense discussion about religion. For the rest of the one-hour flight back to Sacramento we talked about the biblical prophecies promising the second coming of Jesus Christ. He had an amazing recollection of many verses or scriptures, and was almost able to quote the twenty-fourth chapter of Matthew verbatim. We talked about world events that could be considered possible fulfillment of some of the things spoken of by Christ in Matthew 24. He then said something I shall never forget.

"I believe the promise that he will return. I'm convinced the time will come when the entire world will desperately need what His return alone can accomplish."

The chemistry of that moment was very similar to our earlier telephone conversation about prayer. He was speaking in a quiet, contemplative manner. I sensed he was talking to himself as much as to me. In fact, when we landed at Sacramento and were waiting for his limo, he simply put his hand on my shoulder and said, "I really enjoyed the evening. Thanks for listening."

Sometime after that there was another experience, of less than a minute's duration, in which much the same thing happened. It was just after President Nixon's vice president, former Maryland governor Spiro Agnew, had resigned as vice president. There was a great deal of speculation as to whom President Nixon would name to replace Agnew. One of the obvious choices was Ronald Reagan.

Reagan and I were to appear together at a function in Sacramento. I came to his office. We took the elevator down to the garage, and got into the limo for the short trip to our meeting. The conversation turned to Agnew, and I asked Reagan what he thought was the likelihood that he would be asked to assume the office of vice president. His response was spontaneous, nothing staged or rehearsed. He looked down, and then at me. Gesturing upward he simply said, "If He wants me to be the vice president it will happen, and I would have to do it." The "He" in that statement was not Richard Nixon.

There were several experiences with his brother Neil that helped me understand Reagan's faith in God. Once at a reception in California when I was standing in line beside Governor Reagan, someone commented that we looked alike, and in all seriousness asked if I was his brother, Neil. Reagan started to laugh and when he regained his composure he said to me, "Neil is older than I am and looks like he could be your father." Then with a twinkle in his eye he said, "He's also the best friend I ever had."

Neil Reagan had had throat cancer and as often happens in that situation, the surgeons had removed part of his vocal chords. He had been trained to speak again. When he talked it was with a deep husky voice. When I first met Neil he looked me over and in that gravely voice, but with the Reagan twinkle in his eye, said, "Well, there is no doubt you're a conservative."

"How can you tell?" I asked.

"Any man who wears both suspenders and a belt has to be a true conservative," he said.

Later, when Reagan was president, I was with Neil at his home in Rancho Santa Fe, San Diego County, California. As sometimes happened with the two Reagan brothers, in matters of religion they were separate but not divided. Neil was Roman Catholic, while Ronald was Protestant, and during his lifetime affiliated with several different denominations of similar nature.

During this particular visit with Neil I mentioned the fact that through my work with the government of Italy I had arranged for a friend to have an audience with the Pope. Neil looked at me and asked,

"John, could you get me an audience with the Pope?"

"Neil," I said, "your brother appoints the United States ambassador to the Vatican. He is the one who can get you an audience with the Pope. I'll get in touch with him tomorrow."

"Not on your life," Neil rasped. "There is no way on earth I would let him do that. If you can't get me the appointment I don't want it. Under no conditions are you to ask anyone in our government to do that for me."

When he saw my perplexed look he simply said, "Ron would understand that. He's my brother."

We then embarked on a two-hour conversation about Neil and his kid brother. We talked about home life and their times at Eureka College in Illinois. Some of the versions that Neil shared with me regarding events in the life of Ronald Reagan were not entirely consistent with other biographical accounts. According to Neil, he was the one who arranged for his brother to have a screen test while he was in southern California as the radio announcer for a baseball team in spring training. Neil also discussed several items in the career of Ronald Reagan in which Neil was a more active participant than is generally known.

We talked about the bond between them. Neil spoke with wistful nostalgia of the days in Los Angeles when Sunday afternoon meant outdoor barbeques held at the homes of the two brothers. As circumstances changed, the weekly Sunday afternoons in the backyard became once a month, and then just every so often, and finally were at best an annual event, usually associated with birthdays.

The bond between the two brothers was deep and strong. However, I was privy to several experiences demonstrating how each brother was fiercely determined never to be a burden to the other.

Now that Ronald Reagan was President their time together was limited mostly to telephone conversations. Neil came to the first inaugural, but he declined Nancy's invitation to attend the first February birthday party for the President after entering the White House.

I arranged for Neil to have his audience with the Pope through the efforts of Maria Pia Fanfanni, the wife of Aminatori Fanfanni, who had been the Italian Prime Minister on three or four occasions, and was then president of the Italian senate. At the Vatican, while we were waiting for the papal audience to take place, Neil talked of religion and the way the brothers Reagan dealt with it.

"Ron is very deeply religious," he said, "but in a different way than most people. He will listen to a sermon, and then go home and check it out in the Bible himself. He thinks about it, and then decides whether or not it is consistent with his idea about God and the religious life. We don't talk about it often, and now that he's President, we don't get to talk very much at all. But he has told me that after being elected President he has spent more time in prayer than in all of his life before that."

I did not choose to go into the papal reception room with Neil, feeling that it was more appropriate to allow him this privilege with as much privacy as possible. But during that trip to Rome, through the eyes of his brother, I affirmed once again Ronald Reagan's faith in God.

Ed Meese told me that in the nearly thirty years of his relationship with Ronald Reagan, as staff member, cabinet member, family trustee, etc., the subject of Ronald Reagan's religious convictions came up many times when the setting was suitable. "He talked of religion in very comfortable and commonplace terms," Meese said. "For Reagan, a religious overtone in life was so natural and so much a part of his nature that he could refer to religious issues with comfort and without any change of nature or demeanor."

Ronald Reagan's faith was not something his public relations people were allowed to depict or exploit.

It was Reagan's commitment to fundamental principle that set him apart from what he thought was the hypocrisy of the liberal welfare cycle of dependency. Reagan wanted to give people a sense of self-respect and personal achievement. As far as Reagan was concerned, his liberal opponents simply wanted to keep the poor in a state of welfare dependency in order to get their votes.

Critics of Ronald Reagan continually asserted that he was insensitive and unconcerned about those individuals who were destitute, poverty stricken, and educationally disadvantaged. Nothing could be farther from truth. Reagan was always open to any idea that might offer hope and actual benefit to society's downtrodden and forgotten. What Reagan resented and fiercely fought against was the hypocritical and deceitful way in which some liberal politicians raided the public treasury to fund programs that he knew were destined to fail, and repeatedly did fail.

Reagan had no fear of criticizing politicians who through their false promises and ineffective programs helped perpetuate the very evil that they claimed to be fighting. They and the media would revile Reagan because he was no longer willing to allow them to continue keeping the welfare recipient in a state of dependency through government programs that increased taxes, decreased individual freedom and destroyed the ability to rise out of the dependency cycle.

Ronald Reagan was constantly trying to deal with the issue of how to make public welfare more effective in terms of really helping welfare recipients. He regarded the federal and state welfare programs as huge failures because of their tendency to enhance dependency rather than give the welfare recipients incentives to become self sufficient. For Reagan it was not a matter of cutting the dollar cost of welfare, it was a matter of finding a way to lift the welfare-dependent individual out of the sense of hopelessness that was so prevalent among welfare recipients.

In Sacramento, the Church of Jesus Christ of Latter-day Saints maintains a welfare cannery. Members of the church donate their labor to process various products that are grown on church farms. These products are then made available to the needy members of the church primarily within that geographic region served by the cannery. I had explained this program to the Governor, and he asked if we could arrange a time to tour the cannery. The date was set, and on October 10, 1973, we drove out to the cannery.

For an hour and a half he toured the cannery, meeting forty or so volunteers who were working there, including a medical doctor, various other professionals, housewives, and several unemployed individuals who were helping in the cannery while seeking employment. After the tour there was a briefing for the governor explaining how the welfare program of the church actually functioned. The need to provide people with a sense of dignity while they were seeking to reestablish their ability to provide for themselves and their families was discussed at some length.

Reagan was obviously impressed with the program. He asked a number of questions about how needy people responded to the program. He remembered and later quoted to me several times a phrase he heard there: "Our program gives recipients a sense of hope, a sense of self worth, and the skills to become self-sufficient."

When the tour was over Reagan and I spent some time visiting about what he had seen and heard. He was enthusiastic about the possibility of applying the same concepts he had seen at the cannery to the California welfare system. As we talked he made this comment:

"Think what it would mean to the thousands of people who are now being trapped in dependency on state welfare if we could put them into a program like this. Instead of making welfare a hand-out that destroyed self respect and self reliance we would be giving people the ability to achieve the independence that should be the right of every American."

He went on in that same vein for several minutes. He was excited and animated about the possibility of lifting California's welfare recipients out of the dependency rut and into a lifestyle that was productive and would not only feed their bodies but their souls as well.

Several weeks later we happened to be in a meeting with the legislative leaders from the Democratic Party. After describing our experience at the cannery, Reagan then suggested that we work together to draft some legislative proposals that would incorporate the same principles we had seen in action at the cannery. He said,

"I have no doubt that we could get thousands of people to volunteer their time and effort to help prepare food and clothing for the welfare recipients. But more important, with a program like this we can give the welfare recipients the opportunity to actually help earn their own welfare benefits. We can give them the chance to feel that they are not on the dole but are really earning the benefits they receive. Ultimately we can move them out into the job market and they can be fully independent."

Reagan looked at the men to whom he was speaking. Not one of them even offered a comment that the matter was worthy of further study and consideration. Finally, one of the members of the state assembly said, "Governor, you can go ahead and submit it if you want, but I wouldn't hold your breath waiting for anything to happen if I were you."

After the meeting was over and I had returned to my office Reagan called me on the phone.

"What do you think?" he asked. "Can we make something happen with this?"

I responded with my own analysis of why his proposal would not be acceptable to those who used welfare programs to obtain political loyalty and support through economic dependency. "I'm not willing to accept that as a valid reason for not trying," he said. "We're going to create a welfare program that is honorable and fair. I'm not going to abandon those people—and I'm not going to let society absolve its conscience by just raiding the state treasury."

Throughout his time as governor of California Reagan kept trying to find a way to raise the poverty-stricken to a level of dignity and self-respect. He wanted a welfare program that offered them the opportunity to help pay their own way while being prepared to become contributing, fully self-reliant members of the community.

During the decades of the fifties and the sixties the Church of Jesus Christ of Latter-day Saints (Mormon), to which my wife and I belong, had an active program of bringing Native American children from Indian reservations to live with foster families for the duration of the school year. At the end of the school year the child would return to his or her natural family on the reservation. At the beginning of the next school year the process would be repeated.

Our family participated in this program, taking in a young Mojave girl named Esther. She was a delightful child who could run like a deer. One day our oldest son, David, who was the same age as Esther, asked if he could meet Governor Reagan. I promised to see if I could arrange it. Helene Von Dam, the Governor's gracious and long suffering secretary, made the appointment.

The next day, at the appointed hour, I brought the two children to the governor's office. Reagan could not have been more accommodating. He held out the famous jelly bean jar as both children scooped out huge handfuls. We visited for several minutes, and then with a warm handshake and a kind farewell, we departed from the governor's office.

After taking the children home and then returning to my office there was a message for me to call the Governor. He wanted to know more about the foster program for Native Americans. I explained the concept of bringing the children into a family environment that would help them see the world outside the reservation and give them a means to become better integrated into that outside world. Sociologists have long agreed that the major barrier preventing Native American children from escaping the vicious cycle of reservation life is their lack of opportunity to participate in any alternative lifestyle. The purpose of this program was to give the children a better self-image and instill within them the confidence that they could achieve worthy goals outside the cycle of hopelessness that was all too often a part of reservation life.

Reagan became very animated about the idea. The foster family provided all of the financial support for the child during the school year. The home environment was monitored by the Church's social services organization. Even though the bureaucrats had a necessary role, the real service rendered came through the efforts of the volunteer families.

Reagan then began to talk of ways in which this concept could be applied to California's social welfare programs. Why not establish a program whereby a stable family could "adopt" a welfare dependent family? A volunteer program with little interference from government bureaucrats and even less dependency upon the public treasury was exactly what Reagan needed in order to create his vision of a society with maximum individual freedom and equal opportunity.

One day someone informed the Governor that under the state statutes involving matters concerning Native Americans he was to appoint a member of the senate as chairman of the state commission on Indian Affairs. California has more than fifty Indian reservations or rancheros, ranging in size from the very small to the very large. While the federal Bureau of Indian Affairs within the Department of the Interior is considered the primary governmental entity dealing with the Indians, the state also had a role in assisting our Native Americans to achieve their maximum potential.

A member of the Governor's staff came to my office with some documents that the Governor had asked that I read with regard to the state Commission on Indian Affairs. I then had a session with Reagan in which he appealed to me to take the appointment as the chairman of the Commission. At the same time we discussed how to implement into the California welfare system the same principles that were being used by the LDS Church in its Indian placement program. After some further discussion I accepted the appointment, and for the next two years served as the chairman of the California State Commission on Indian Affairs while still serving in the senate.

On Monday, February 8, 1971, I had taken a late afternoon flight from Sacramento to Burbank in order to keep an early morning speaking commitment. I slept that night at the home of my wife's parents in Burbank. The next morning, just as I was getting ready to take a shower I heard a strange noise like an ocean wave coming ashore. Suddenly the house lurched, and I saw the entire contents of the medicine cabinet standing in mid-air. Then they all fell into the sink below. It was my first experience with a major earthquake, which came to be known as the San Fernando earthquake of 1971. The entire house had moved eighteen inches so quickly that everything on shelves was momentarily left in mid-air, before falling to the floor.

I rushed to my district office, which was on the eighth floor of the Glendale Federal Building. There was a scene of total chaos. Amazingly, the telephones were still working. One of the first calls informed me that a tragedy of major proportions had taken place at the veterans hospital in the north end of the valley, and located within my senatorial district. Leaving the mess in the office for the staff to deal with I drove alone out to the veterans hospital.

The building that had taken the worst damage was an old four story structure, built in the early 1920's. Just after I arrived two other men also arrived—Governor Ronald Reagan, and the Sheriff of Los Angeles County, Peter Pitchess. The Governor asked me to join them as the three of us began a tour of the damaged facilities. One of the senior administrators led the way.

There was visible damage to many of the structures. There were emergency fire department crews working at several sites, but the area of primary focus was the totally collapsed four story building. The three of us, plus the hospital administrator, stood silently as we watched the rescue crews uncover an old World War I veteran in a pile of rubble. For him the long lonely wait of his mortal probation was over. In all, some forty-six men died when the earthquake collapsed the upper stories down into the first floor.

The rescue crews placed the body of the veteran on a stretcher about ten feet in front of us. The hospital administrator was able to identify the body and came back to us with some brief details about the man. He had been alone at the facility for nearly a year. No one had come to see him. When the earthquake hit he had been asleep in his small room. Beyond that no one knew much about him.

Reagan's reaction became one of those spontaneous moments that you could never anticipate and probably never hope to see again. He was emotionally moved, and while Sheriff Pitchess and I sensed the solemnity of the moment, Reagan seemed to see it in a much broader concept with regard to a nation's debt to those who had served in its armed forces. As we watched the rescue crews madly searching for other victims, Reagan began to talk about what he called ...*these forgotten old men*. As other bodies were pulled from the rubble the Governor, almost as though the sheriff and I were not present, spoke in a low and emotional voice of how the nation had forgotten those who had faithfully and willingly gone forth in uniform to secure our heritage of freedom.

"How could they be left alone?" he said. "Why wasn't there someone who could come and befriend them, to honor them for the service and sacrifice they had so honorably rendered?"

We remained together for over an hour as we toured the damage to the rest of the facility. Sheriff Pitchess had other problems to deal with, a freeway that had collapsed and some looting was taking place at damaged businesses. As the governor and I walked about for a final assessment of the damage, he continued to express his feelings. What seemed to trouble him the most was that some obscure old man who had gone forth in defense of his fellow Americans had been totally forgotten. Now he lay dead, his body crumpled and crushed and covered with dirt and dust, the memory of his life and service now extinct except for the two of us.

Other bodies were laid out on the ground, covered with blankets or already tightly encased in body bags. We stood silently observing them, and then I saw Reagan do something that was a defining moment in my relationship with him. There were tears in his eyes as he straightened to attention, slowly bringing his right arm to a military salute, holding that position for just a few moments, before turning and walking slowly to his waiting car. That salute was done spontaneously, with a genuine sense of gratitude and love. I wished with all my heart that those whose lifeless bodies lay before us had been allowed to take one last look at that farewell tribute before moving on to their new destiny.

Bill Clark, the president's deputy Secretary of State and then National Security Advisor told me that Reagan had a very deep and personal sense of affection for those who had served the nation in the military. He was especially conscious of those who had given their lives in service to the nation. Ed Meese recalled that when the bodies of the Marines killed in the terrorist bombing at Beirut, Lebanon, in 1983 were flown home to Dover Air Force Base, Reagan was anxious to be present and to be able to express both condolence, and if possible, comfort to the families of those who died. He felt deep sorrow for those families and wanted to find some way to personally express his concern for their sense of loss in the deaths of these Marines.

Ed Meese accompanied Reagan to meet the flight. Meese recalled:

"The only time that I saw him really saddened was when I went with him to Dover Air Force Base to meet the families of the Marines who were killed in the terrorist bombing in Beirut, in 1983. It was a very difficult time for him personally. He deeply empathized with the families. It reminded me of how President Lincoln would go down to the telegraph office at the War Department to read the names of those killed in action and then frequently write personal letters of condolence to the families."

I asked Ed for other examples of Reagan's empathy for others. He noted the following:

"He was always worried about staff members going home to be with their families. It was very important to him that the loyalty and dedication of the staff members not be allowed to potentially destroy their family life. He was conscious of many of their personal problems and tried to be aware of when and how they needed special help.

"It was very difficult for him to discharge someone who either was not performing up to the required standard or who for some other reason had to be let go. If he had to let someone go he always tried to do it in a way that let them save face, that minimized the embarrassment or negative reflection on the person.

"He was a man of great empathy and compassion. He did a lot of things very quietly for other people. He would get a letter from someone who was in need—and he would call one of his friends. Frank Sinatra was often a secret benefactor at Reagan's request. I know of situations where the Governor personally or through someone like Frank Sinatra would take care of a situation in which someone suffered a loss. Once he heard of a little boy whose bicycle was stolen. He arranged for a new bike to be delivered, but it was done anonymously.

"A soldier wrote a letter from Vietnam addressed to 'The Governor of California.' He had just gotten married before being sent to Vietnam. He sent the letter with some money, in which he asked the governor to please arrange to have some flowers sent to his wife for their first anniversary. So Reagan personally went out and bought the flowers and delivered them to the lady.

"He would see something in the paper that he thought was meritorious and he would call the person on the telephone to thank them for what they had done. On one occasion he called a man to express appreciation, and after introducing himself as Ronald Reagan the man responded, 'Yea, and I'm the Queen of England', and hung up on him. Reagan laughed as he recited this conversation to his staff.

"He was never jealous of other people who were achieving things in the political process that he might have wanted to accomplish. He had a great regard for Nixon. He was deeply disappointed that Nixon had to resign. He regarded the entire Watergate situation as a real tragedy—that it was too bad that a man who had so much to offer the nation was forced to resign from office. Under the circumstances it might have been tempting for him to take pleasure in Nixon's demise, particularly since it was conceivable that it would aid his own presidential ambitions. That was never the case. He never begrudged the success of others, and often felt very deeply the sorrow of a personal tragedy, such as Nixon's resignation."

I have attempted to present here some of the experiences that confirmed the reality that Ronald Reagan was both a man of faith and a man of charity. As I re-read these pages I feel a sense of personal disappointment that they are not more effective in conveying the depth of both of these qualities as I knew them to exist in this man. Honorable men do not parade their virtues or solicit commendation by making certain that others see and know of their good works and charity.

Through the years of our association, with a comment, a gesture of the hand, or the facial expression, he communicated both faith and charity. It happened in the privacy of an automobile ride, or during a late night flight, or in his own home where he usually shared these values. The language came naturally, unrehearsed and unintended for posterity, simply a spontaneous expression of his personal feelings.

NINE

INTELLECT

I have never understood why so many commentators and authors underestimate Ronald Reagan's mind. On many occasions I watched him listen to a thirty minute briefing regarding some complex facet of state government, and then go into an expanded meeting with the legislative leaders or the media and deal with those same issues as though he was as familiar with them as the experts who had briefed him. It was not simply a matter of immediate recall of something which was soon forgotten. Weeks later, without any further review of the material, he could still engage in a thoroughly detailed discussion of the issues involved.

In 1972 we had several meetings in January and February regarding the state budget. Even though Reagan still had three years left in his second term, he seemed to sense the approaching end of his time as Governor. He began to refer more often to his *legacy* as the Governor, and more and more he expressed concern how his decisions would effect the people of California after he was no longer in the Governor's chair.

One area of intense focus was the matter of our annual state budgets. Reagan wanted to put in place a series of budgets that would effectively confirm in future years his philosophy of limited government intervention in the lives of the people and limited government regulation of the economic process.

After introducing his budget to the legislature there were meetings with the legislative leadership, including the chairmen of the senate and assembly committees that worked on the budget. These men were involved in budget issues every day. They understood the budget details as much as anyone in the Governor's administration.

On Monday, March 20, the Governor invited the Republican legislative leaders to come to his office for another briefing on the budget. After the briefing and a question and answer session with the director of finance, the Democratic legislative leaders and respective committee chairmen who had power over the budget process would then join us. In these sessions it was easy to see the facility of Reagan's mind at work.

The director of finance gave us a one hour briefing on the revenue forecast for the state, and the details of the budget. Reagan was insisting on finding more areas to cut, squeeze, and trim, although what that actually meant was not a lower budget than the prior year, but a budget with less increase than in the past. He was very much involved in probing various areas of the budget where we could find a way to do more with less.

When the meeting was expanded to include the Democratic leadership, the Governor chaired the meeting and presented his defense of the proposed budget. As the Governor began making his presentation the two respective committee chairman attempted to distract him by raising extraneous issues that supposedly had a negative impact on what Reagan was proposing. Reagan never faltered in maintaining his composure and staying focused on his objective for the meeting. He seemed unconcerned about whether or not they agreed with him, or whether or not they accepted his proposals. His basic thrust was to make it clear to all assembled what he intended to accomplish with the budget.

As the session went on Reagan demonstrated his phenomenal

ability to recall and explain the volumes of information presented in earlier briefings as he fielded the questions and objections presented by the Democratic attendees. He seldom turned to his director of finance or to other staff people for answers. He deftly countered arguments based on data, sometimes actually correcting inaccurate details in the comments of those questioning him. The meeting was intense, the atmosphere a confrontation of wills, and through it all he remained the composed unflappable individual I had known for ten years.

I noted in the prior chapter that Reagan was frequently accused of being insensitive to the needs of welfare recipients. Nothing could have been farther from the truth. In all of these meetings he was constantly asking how we could replace the sterility of government welfare payments with meaningful programs that would emancipate the welfare recipient from a life of dependency. He knew the budgetary details in the various programs involving welfare recipients. He continually challenged the prevailing wisdom about how welfare programs should function. He was constantly alert to any concept that might make the funds being expended capable of doing more good in the lives of the recipients. As our Democratic counterparts assailed the proposed budget items involving welfare programs, the Governor skillfully and successfully defended the proposals contained in the budget. His antagonists were not intellectual lightweights, and yet they never seemed to get the Governor over a barrel as they battled over welfare funding.

I saw this aspect of Ronald Reagan's intellectual and moral leadership on many occasions. He displayed an incredible capacity to remain absolutely unyielding in his convictions and his objectives, but was never offensive or defiant towards others. He would listen attentively to the alternative argument, and then respond with a clear and often detailed explanation of why that was not consistent with his intent regarding a specific issue or the course of state government in general. When the exchange was finished there was never a sense of acrimony in what he had done, but also never any doubt in the minds of everyone present as to what the Governor wanted to accomplish.

As I have reflected back on these experiences in watching Ronald Reagan interact with others of differing philosophy and values, I marvel again at the combination of qualities that made him so effective as a leader. He had a very penetrating mind, and anyone who claims otherwise never knew or saw Ronald Reagan in the arena of intellectual confrontation.

On February 19, 2001, Lady Margaret Thatcher, the former prime minister of Great Britain, gave a speech in Fort Myers, Florida, at a Hillsdale College seminar. In that speech she reminisced about experiences with world leaders during the time she was the prime minister. Two contemporary world leaders at the time were Ronald Reagan and the general secretary of the Soviet Union, Michail Gorbachev. Lady Thatcher made this comment about her experiences with Ronald Reagan:

"It always fascinated me that people thought Ronnie Reagan was not a detail man. If ever he was negotiating or going on a significant visit, he would have everything at his fingertips. He was the most thorough person in preparation that I ever knew. And of course those he met with were always most impressed. He knew the answers, and would have a whole range of questions himself. President Reagan could dominate any meeting between two people. He's a very, very great man, and we're very fortunate that we had him when we did, because I think if it hadn't been for him, we would not have begun to get the cracking up of the Soviet Union."

Reagan's intellectual capabilities were especially evident in discussions about taxation and the state budget. He majored in economics at Eureka College, and he was continually reading about the various consequences of taxation upon economic progress and prosperity. He frequently quoted various authors when making comments on taxation. He was firmly convinced that the ability to tax is the ability to destroy. After several years as Governor he became convinced that all large bureaucracies had insatiable appetites for money. More and more he became determined to limit government funding to items and programs essential to the welfare of the entire body politic. I heard him on several occasions quote from such diverse individuals as the Roman emperor Diocletion and the nation's first secretary of the treasury, Alexander Hamilton, to the effect that "...governments always begin with low taxes and high revenue and then go to high taxes with low revenue."

Long before he arrived in Washington, Ronald Reagan had a clear picture of the necessity to prevent the tax burden from depressing the economy. He learned as Governor that if he could reduce the tax burden he would actually increase the tax revenue because of the increased prosperity it would produce.

Reagan's intellectuality was amply demonstrated at the various governors' conferences. He did not need to seek out media opportunities at these events. He always seemed to be in the center of national interest and the working press were always trying to find a way to interview him. He attended these conferences determined to learn from them and find things other governors were doing that he could apply in California. Yet, the media clamor was a constant distraction from his desire to listen and learn, and also took away his preparation time for the panel discussions.

At one particular conference he was assigned to a panel regarding a regional electricity distribution grid. It was a complex issue, and before leaving California he had spent several hours being briefed on the technical challenges of the regional distribution of electricity and the economics involved. At the conference he had scheduled the hour before the panel discussion to review his briefing papers. Somehow a commitment was made for a media interview at the very time he was supposed to be free to review his notes. It meant he would go into the panel discussion having had only a very few minutes to review his notes. However, he opted to keep the appointment that had been made for the interview. It took most of the hour he had set aside for his preparation.

On the panel were two of his fellow governors who had been deeply involved with this issue and had made an extensive study of the problems and proposed solutions. Reagan took his assigned place on the panel, and for the next two hours skillfully participated in both his presentation and the question and answer session. He was not attempting to upstage anyone, but it was obvious from the demeanor of the audience that it was Reagan's presentation that received the most attention. In the question and answer session he demonstrated his intellectual capacity to recall specific technical details and apply them to hypothetical situations that were presented in the questions.

Reagan had a vast knowledge of history and the insightful statements of political philosophers of the past. Ed Meese recalled that:

"Reagan laughed at being described as an intellectual lightweight. He really did not let this type of criticism bother him. He had no time for the supercilious elitists—those who were so impressed with themselves. He loved to visit with authors and commentators like Bill Buckley about profound issues. But Reagan was frequently bored by so-called intellectuals who wanted to impress him with erudite opinions they felt needed to be heard. After giving the individual an appropriately polite audience Reagan would make whatever comment necessary to essentially shut the person off so he could move on to something else.

"He never pretended to be an intellectual, but he had a great intellectual capacity in terms of reading, retention, assimilation of ideas and facts. He would usually study something that had a purpose and not just something that was interesting for its own sake."

"He studied very carefully that which he needed to know. He had a great deal of intellectual curiosity about those things that were interesting or important for him to understand in his official capacity."

As a university student my major course of study was history. Thus I had some acquaintance with the political leaders and philosophers of the past. Several times in meetings Reagan would illustrate a concept by quoting from or citing the example of a leader or philosopher from ancient Greece or Rome, from the renaissance period in Europe or a more modern writer. It was amusing to watch the countenances of many in the room, as their brows would furrow and they would look at each other trying to remember who Diocletion was, or what it was that John Locke wrote about, or who it was that wrote the fiftieth Federalist Paper.

The Federalist Papers were of particular interest to Reagan in his personal reading and research. He yearned to implement government as the founding fathers had intended, on both a national and state level. He was comfortable talking about the American Constitution in relation to a proposed or existing government program. He worked hard to obtain his knowledge of political history, and he memorized many quotations and details for the speeches he began giving in the mid-fifties.

For more than thirty years Ronald Reagan searched history for answers and solutions to the social and economic issues of his time. When he found answers he was tenacious in applying them in his public life.

As Ed Meese noted above, Ronald Reagan didn't care what other people thought about his intellectual capacity. He was never concerned about how others would rank him among the elite or intelligentsia of his day. He did care intensely about how to deal with issues that had perplexed and eluded his predecessors, as Governor and as President.

When he became Governor there was a huge deficit and an approaching tidal wave of unfunded obligations. When he left the Governor's office the state had a significant cash surplus and was in the midst of a solid economic recovery. He became President when the nation was floundering in an economic and social morass, and our foreign relations was at an all time low. He left office having put in motion the forces that ended forty years of the Cold War. He was the most admired man in the free world. The nation's economy was thriving in the midst of unprecedented prosperity.

The self-anointed pseudo-intellectual commentators would have Americans believe that all of these achievements were simply the result of incredible luck. These are the same people who spend their lives plastered with makeup, standing in front of cameras reading from tele-prompters what others have written about people and places whose names they have to be taught to pronounce.

That these oracles of the media could denigrate Ronald Reagan's achievements, while never accomplishing anything themselves, did not bother him. After all, he too had once earned his livelihood as an actor.

TEN

THE REAGAN AMENDMENT

As he came closer and closer to the end of his second term as governor of California, Ronald Reagan became more and more concerned about how to ensure that future administrations and legislatures would not be able to plunge the state back into the same fiscal morass that had existed when he was first elected in 1966. As he labored with each annual budget and had seen the insatiable appetite of the state bureaucracies for increased funding, Reagan began to talk about finding a way to place a limit on what the government could take from the people. He wanted to limit the ability of government to take whatever it wanted.

Ed Meese recalled Reagan's concerns very vividly. He said:

"The Governor always talked about the fact that government would tax to get whatever it wanted, not what it needed. It was a theme in his private conversations. He was convinced that both the state and the federal government would continue to increase the tax burden upon the people unless there was some way to limit what the government could take from them."

The Governor explored a variety of taxation concepts that could possibly accomplish this goal. On two occasions I met with him and a Professor Smith, from one of the California universities, regarding a value-added tax concept that the professor had developed. Professor Smith had spent considerable time making an extensive study of the application of a value-added tax in California, and argued that such a tax would accomplish what the Governor wanted to do.

Reagan spent considerable time studying Professor Smith's ideas. He asked a lot of detailed questions that reflected how intensely he had studied the over-all issue of tax limitation. In the end Reagan decided that the value-added tax concept was not the answer he was seeking.

After the failure of the anti-obscenity proposition that I had sponsored for the 1972 November ballot, Reagan asked me to meet with him regarding the entire process involved with qualifying our proposition for the ballot. As noted earlier, in an impossibly short period of time we had mobilized thousands of volunteers to carry our petitions door to door in order to obtain the necessary one million signatures of registered voters required to put the matter on the ballot. Reagan was fascinated with how we accomplished that task, and was obviously becoming more and more determined to take to the people a proposal to deal with the issue of future tax increases.

The Governor finally determined how to protect the people from excessive tax increases should future administrations and legislatures want to dramatically increase the state's budget and or its bonded indebtedness. With the active participation of several highly qualified economists and experts in both taxation and constitutional law, Reagan proposed an amendment for the state constitution and circulated it to members of the legislature. At the same time, he initiated a very intense effort across the state to circulate the petitions for signatures to enable the matter to be placed on the next election ballot.

The amendment illustrated Reagan's core philosophy of limiting the power of government to invade the financial resources of the population. Essentially, the Governor proposed an upper limit on the percentage of the state's annual gross product that could be taken by the state in taxes. Having campaigned on a promise to cut, squeeze, and trim the state budget, Governor Reagan had been forced to ask for the largest tax increase in the history of the state in order to keep the state functioning. The proposed constitutional amendment made certain that future legislatures and future governors would not be able to throttle the state's economic growth with a tax burden that would destroy the ability of business to create new jobs.

The amendment qualified for the ballot through the efforts of thousands of volunteers throughout the state. Reagan received conflicting advice from his staff and Republican leaders about when to schedule the election on the ballot proposition. Reagan's staff wanted a special November election called by the Governor just for the ballot measure. The legislative leaders urged him to wait until June of 1974, when voters would be turning out to vote in record numbers for the state's primary elections. The staff members won the debate and the Governor called a special election in November of 1973 for the sole purpose of voting for the constitutional amendment.

In September Reagan held a meeting in his office with the legislative leaders of both parties. His purpose was to defuse the partisanship that was dominating the public debate about the proposed amendment. The Governor was genuinely convinced that a number of the legislative leaders from the Democratic Party would give their support to the ballot proposition if they only understood it. For over an hour he engaged in a very detailed explanation of the economic benefit to the state by having the tax limitation included in the state constitution.

One of the key provisions in the amendment made it possible in a situation of legitimate necessity for the people to approve taxes exceeding the limitations of the formula. As Governor Reagan attempted to explain this process one of the democratic legislative leaders, Assemblyman Jack Fenton said to Reagan, "Since the people have not been intelligent enough to vote for other needed taxes submitted to them on the ballot, what makes you think they would be intelligent or enlightened enough to vote for increasing the tax limit you are proposing?"

It was the only occasion I could remember ever seeing Ronald Reagan left speechless. He looked at Fenton for what seemed like several minutes without saying a word. Finally he responded,

"Well Jack, I think we just have to have faith in the ability of the people to discern what needs to be done."

Later Reagan asked me, "Did he really say that? Is it possible for anyone to be that arrogant?" Reagan was dumbfounded that an elected representative of the people was so contemptuous of the ability of the people to deal with the issues of state. He could only shake his head in dismay that there was such an attitude of superior wisdom among those who dealt on a daily basis with the life, liberty, and property of twenty-five million Americans.

I participated in those meetings for many months. The genius of the proposal had become clear to those who wrestled each day with the reality of keeping the state treasury from being emptied by liberal elitists who knew all the answers regarding how to best provide for the public welfare. But they didn't know anything about giving incentives to business to hire more employees to make profits marketing goods and services in order to pay the heavy state tax burden that hampered economic growth even under Ronald Reagan.

Our counterparts on the other side of the isle refused to accept any of Reagan's well-researched data showing how the implementation of his proposal would actually increase state revenue through the increased economic prosperity that it would bring to the state.

The election turned into a partisan contest in which the speaker of the state assembly, Robert Moretti, championed the cause of the state teachers union arguing that the amendment would only lead to the loss of state and local benefits and services. Reagan worked intensely to get the message through to the people about how the proposal would assure a brighter economic future for California.

On October 19, in San Francisco, he gave a solid defense of the proposal before the Commonwealth Club. Again on October 24, he did much the same thing before the elected officials at the annual meeting of the League of California Cities, also meeting in San Francisco.

Several weeks prior to his speech at the Commonwealth Club, the speaker of the state assembly, Robert Moretti, who skillfully used the election on the Reagan amendment as a means of furthering his own ambitions to become Governor, had spoken to this same group. In his talk Moretti had wildly distorted both the substance and the effect of *Proposition I*. In response Reagan said:

"He explained it with all the enthusiasm George III would have used in interpreting the Declaration of Independence. It is absolutely untrue, however, that if *Proposition I* passes it will rain on all the Forty-Niner home games. That is about the only thing our opponents have not said would happen."

On a more serious note the Governor then said,

"I expected a battle over this proposal to limit taxes, but even so, I am afraid I was not prepared for the shrill hysteria and ferocity of those who rallied to protect their place at the public trough. They have resorted to falsehood, distortion, and scare tactics claiming all kinds of dire results if this limitation plan should be approved, even though the specifics of the plan actually make impossible the things they say will happen."

Reagan then gave a summary of his efforts during the prior seven years as Governor.

"As you are well aware, ours has not been known as a spendthrift administration. Seven years ago when we started, I had a belief that government could be run on the same rules and principles that apply to the running of a business or even a home. That belief has been confirmed. We have *cut, squeezed and trimmed.* When there were surpluses as a result of those cuts we returned those surpluses to the people in the form of bonuses or rebates. Now it has become politically impossible to reduce taxes on an ongoing basis. But we have not neglected those functions which are properly government's responsibility."

The Governor then recited a long list of state-supported functions that had received significant increases in their appropriations during his term, including a nearly one hundred percent increase in state support of public education during his administration. He then said:

"None of these increases in spending met with resistance (from the Democrats in the legislature). But the economies that made these increases possible were opposed vehemently, and our rebates of the surpluses brought hysterical charges that fiscal chaos would be the result of such foolishness."

Reagan was proud of the reforms he made in the state's welfare system. He turned to a recital of those reforms as a means of confirming his faith that the Reagan Amendment would effectively prevent unwarranted increases in taxes or bring about the dire consequences to other programs that opponents had claimed.

"Before we got too upset with the dire predictions some say will follow passage of *Proposition 1,* maybe we had better recall what the same people were saying about our welfare reforms and how catastrophe would follow their adoption. Our own welfare caseload was increasing by 40,000 a month when we started our reforms. Today, there are 365,000 fewer people on welfare. We did not have a $700 million tax increase or deficit—we had a surplus. County relief went down, not up. Forty two counties reduced their basic property taxes last year and forty five have done so this year…I make no apology for wanting California to be first in reducing taxes, systematically and permanently, without curtailing essential services or denying government new revenues for meeting new problems that might arise in the future."

Reagan then turned to the fundamental philosophical commitment that was the real engine driving his determination to give the people of California a constitutional shield against increasing taxes and future spendthrift legislatures.

"There is a fundamental philosophy over the role government is supposed to play in the lives of our people. On November 6, we will be choosing between government by the consent of the people and government ruling the people through the power of taxation…For two generations we have been drifting toward almost total government control of our economic life because government has been taking a larger and larger percentage of the people's income.

"I have been asked why should I be so concerned? After all, federal and local taxes take most of it, far more than the state does. That is true. But I am not in the federal government, or in local government. I am part of the government of California. So what is wrong with doing something to slow down the growth of big government at the state level?

"Why should government be permitted the unlimited power to increase taxes faster than the increase in your earnings? For twenty years or so, California's total earnings have increased seven and one half percent a year. State government costs have gone up ten percent each year.

"Proposition 1 may be a new and radical idea to politicians, but it should not be to you. Every day of your life you have to live within your income or go bankrupt. Government has been balancing its budget by unbalancing yours."

There were two themes that appeared frequently in Ronald Reagan's private discussions about the role of government. One was the critical need for the supremacy of law and not the caprice of the rule of men in governing the lives of the people. The second theme was his conviction that the federal constitution was a document inspired of God to assure the protection of the freedom of the individual. He turned to both of those themes in defense of *Proposition 1*.

"This is not some radical hair-brain scheme marking a departure from our representative form of government. It makes no change whatsoever in the balance between the branches of government. It is a restoration of our traditional concept of constitutional government, wherein the people ensure that we are governed by laws, not by men. Was it Burke who said: 'Never give any power to your best friend that you wouldn't give to your worst enemy?' Our founding fathers told us not to place our trust in men, but to bind their hands with the chains of a constitution."

The next paragraph is one that reflected Ronald Reagan's magnificent ability to communicate. One had to be present and actually hear him deliver the following paragraph to appreciate the impact it would have on the audience. It was not only the words that he spoke but the spirit in which he delivered those words that confirmed for the audience the truth and the reality of what he said.

"Have we forgotten in these decades of more and more government that government can have no power except that voluntarily granted it by the people? Did the people ever intend that government should have the right to all we earn? Have the people so lost confidence in their ability to govern themselves that they are willing to give that power to some chosen elite in the marble halls of government?"

In his speech of a week later to the annual meeting of the League of California Cities, the Governor concluded with a final appeal.

"Never has an issue been more clearly drawn. On one side are those who react hysterically at the thought of anyone threatening their place at the trough. On the other side are the people—those we serve—caught up in a spiral of higher and higher prices they did not cause and cannot cure. And by far the highest cost item in their entire budget is the cost of government.

"*Proposition 1* is a tax cut, beginning January 1, with continuing cuts over a period of years. *Proposition 1* gives to the people the right to say to state government, 'Above that percentage of our earning you presently take in taxes, you cannot go without our permission.' Provision is made for emergencies. Protection is given to other levels of government.

"A yes vote will serve notice that the people do care and even the tax eaters in those puzzle palaces on the Potomac will have to take heed. Government has never before offered its people such an opportunity. I hope you will decide to be a part of this. There may never be another chance."

In chapter six I made reference to the Public Broadcasting Network program of the 1970's entitled *The Advocates*. In late October of 1973, just before the November election which Governor Reagan had called to vote on *Proposition I*, the only issue on the ballot, the directors of *The Advocates* produced and broadcast a one-hour program on the issue of the Reagan amendment.

On that program, which was broadcast nationwide on the night of October 31, 1973, I was the affirmative advocate, and my two witnesses in support of the Reagan amendment were Governor Ronald Reagan and Dr. Milton Freedman.

As my first witness, I asked Governor Reagan what was wrong with big government, why was it so dangerous? He responded as follows:

"When government gets too big, freedom is lost.

Government is supposed to be the servant. But when a government can tax the people with no limit or no restraint on what the government can take, then the government has become the master. Government's track record at problem solving is not all that good. Far too often, government does not solve the problem, but simply subsidizes it."

I then asked the Governor to explain how the Reagan amendment would help solve that problem. He responded in these words:

"Well, we think that we are proposing an economic bill of rights for every working man and woman in California. We will limit the percentage of the people's earnings that the government can spend, and yet the limit will be high enough that it will sustain the present level of government services with the additional money needed to meet the cost of inflation and population increase, and with additional funding for new or expanded government programs. At the same time, we will reduce all of the taxes over a period of years without reducing government services."

The next question was designed to address one of the issues being raised in objection to the Reagan amendment. "Governor, why a constitutional amendment? Can't you and the state legislature solve this problem?" Here Reagan responded with the background of seven years of struggling to keep the legislature from appropriating the state back into the situation of near bankruptcy that existed when he was first elected.

"Well, the record speaks for itself. Apparently the legislature can't. If I had signed all of the spending bills that have been sent to my desk in the last seven years, billions of dollars in spending bills, the budget of California today would be more than (thirty percent) above its present level. The state sales tax would have to be nearly double what it is now, and the personal income tax would have to be two and one-half times what it presently is.

"Why a constitutional amendment? Because that is what the constitution is for. When government has broken beyond the bounds of restraint, when government is imposing unjustly on the people, then you need to have a constitutional amendment so that the people can take back that power into their own hands."

Another argument being made against the Reagan amendment was that it would emasculate the power of the legislature. In response to this issue Reagan said:

"Not at all. The amendment makes one change, and one change only—it places a limit on the amount of money the government can tax. From there on the legislature is in total control of the manner of spending, the tax structure—the legislature can raise taxes, can lower taxes, can cancel taxes, it can pass new taxes, it can close loopholes."

The Reagan amendment contained a mechanism for dealing with emergency situations, which the governor explained as follows:

"There is a provision in the measure for the legislature to have access to an emergency fund, a very sizeable fund, so that in the event of an economic emergency or a natural disaster the legislature can use that fund. Beyond that, the legislature is given the power to raise taxes above the constitutional limit to meet any valid emergency."

Reagan responded to other issues, such as the heavy-handed tactic of state governments to shift service burdens to local government without providing the funds to pay the cost of the service. But his most telling arguments were in support of the premise that it was clear from the performance of the legislature (and the congress) that there was neither the political will nor the personal integrity in the legislative bodies to exercise the discipline necessary to prevent the government from becoming an oppressive master through the power of unlimited taxation.

In the end, the decision to call a special election in November of 1973 instead of waiting for the June ballot of 1974 proved to be a serious tactical error. In a massive outlay of money and human resources the teachers' union, much of organized labor, and the welfare recipients were able to defeat the proposal. For Reagan it was his most bitter political defeat during his eight years as Governor.

Reagan's assurance that the state's economy would actually experience substantial growth under the amendment was never believed. Ironically, it was later as president that he was able to prove that his economic theory was correct. It was that verification of his faith in the critical need to limit the power of government to tax away the creative and entrepreneurial spirit of the people that brought him the most satisfaction at the end of his first four-year term as President.

In a post-election conversation I asked Reagan if he would try again to get the amendment adopted. He said, "No, there simply isn't the time nor is there the political will among our own supporters to try again." Then he paused for a moment, and speaking reflectively he said, "I would really have liked it to be my epitaph as Governor. Nothing else I could have done for the people of California would have been as important as the passage of that proposal."

The Governor often thought of California as a microcosm of the nation as a whole. He frequently voiced the idea that if we could bring about a change in the pattern of tax, tax, spend, spend in California it would make it possible to do the same thing for the entire country. Ronald Reagan viewed the adoption of the Sixteenth Amendment, the graduated income tax, as the creation of the ultimate Frankenstein monster. From the time of the adoption of the Sixteenth Amendment the federal dinosaur has had an insatiable appetite. The growth in federal spending has exceeded what even the most fearful opponents of the Sixteenth Amendment considered possible.

Ronald Reagan often spoke about and quoted from the writings of political philosophers and scholars regarding the fact that the ability to tax in the hands of an unresponsive or irresponsible government could destroy a nation. He would frequently quote Alexander Hamilton's warning that the Republic would be devastated when the people realized they could vote themselves money out of the national treasury. The Governor was convinced that if he could place in the state's constitution a control mechanism over the potential growth of the tax burden the resultant economic prosperity would do more for the most economically deprived of California's citizens than any possible form of government assistance or largesse.

In many of the speeches that he made during his last term as Governor, Reagan would say that the nation had long since reached the point where our national tax policy had become so counter productive to economic growth that it represented the biggest single deterrent to national prosperity. He felt that it was impossible to measure the real cost of our tax burden, in terms of jobs not created and businesses and investments that were taken offshore because of the myopic and irresponsible approach to increased taxation by the national government. He often said, "Our tax policies have become the quicksand that is suffocating the American dream."

In 1990 President George Bush rescinded his "read my lips, no new taxes" commitment made during the 1988 campaign for President. That year I was an unsuccessful candidate for Congress. In response to the Bush tax increase I proposed an adaptation of Ronald Reagan's proposed amendment to the California state constitution for the federal constitution. Because I knew that President Reagan did not want to be perceived as criticizing his successor I referred to the proposal as *The Franklin Amendment*, based on a quote from Benjamin Franklin to the effect that the new constitution had given the American people "...a republic, if you can keep it."

I asked President Reagan for his endorsement of the proposal which he graciously provided. In his letter of endorsement he wrote as follows:

> "I congratulate you on your efforts to reaffirm the principles of a responsible and responsive federal government which was envisioned by the Founding Fathers.
>
> "As you have pointed out, the requirement of a fiscally responsible government with limited powers was deemed essential to the concept of *ordered liberty*. Your constitutional amendment to protect the nation's fiscal integrity and to make the national government more responsive to the people is an important contribution to the preservation of our Republic.
>
> "Your fine work in this endeavor is typical of the public service you rendered when we worked together in California, where you served so well as my Lieutenant Governor. I am pleased that you are continuing your dedication to our country.
>
> "Nancy joins me in wishing you every continued success.
> Sincerely,
> (Signed) Ron"

Thomas Jefferson, in writing his own epitaph, declined to include the fact that he had been president of the United States. Rather, he took greater pride in his authorship of the *Declaration of Independence* as his most notable legacy of public service. Ronald Reagan said to me that he had hoped his amendment to the California state constitution would be his epitaph as Governor. Had he been able to do so I am convinced nothing from his public service would be more pleasing to him than to have it noted that he was the author of the *Reagan Amendment* by which both the California and the national government's fiscal house was finally made a "house of order."

ELEVEN

A MAN WHO CHANGED THE WORLD

"Where there is no vision, the people perish."
(Proverbs 29:18)

Being a man of principle, Ronald Reagan was able to accomplish things other presidents only dreamed about. He won the Cold War with a total and complete victory over the Soviet Union. He did it because he had a vision, because he was a man of courage, unafraid to stand alone, because he was a man of intellect and wisdom, because he was a man of strength and faith. He brought to pass what many consider the single most important political event of the Twentieth Century.

Ed Meese summed it up succinctly this way:

"To get a little bit of a perspective on how things were in 1980, to fully appreciate the policy changes that brought an end to the Cold War, it is important to look back at the situation that Ronald Reagan faced when he took office on the January 21, 1981. It is hard to remember in some way how bad things were, particularly in the national security field.

"We had an underfunded military at the time. There were serious questions about whether the military could be properly used with the syndrome from Vietnam still hanging over us.

"In terms of foreign policy, we had an acquiescence to perpetual coexistence with the Soviet Union, and an acceptance of the inevitable continuance, if not triumph, of socialism as an economic doctrine, and Marxist totalitarianism as a political doctrine.

"Bleak as that was, the intelligence situation was not much better. Indeed, it was perhaps even worse."

It is ironic that the people who gave America that set of circumstances described by Meese are the same ones who now insist that the Cold War ended in spite of Ronald Reagan, not because of him. However, their own words spoken and printed during the same time that Reagan was instituting the policies that won the Cold War clearly show both their hypocrisy and error.

Job said, "...oh, that mine adversary had written a book." (Job 31:35) Since the end of the Cold War Ronald Reagan's adversaries have gone to every possible extreme to establish that he had nothing to do with the end of the Cold War. The problem for them is that during the time Ronald Reagan was telling the nation that we could win the Cold War with the Soviet Union his liberal adversaries are all on record telling the world that the Soviet Union was unassailably strong. Reagan's critics refused to participate in the ultimate victory of the West in the Cold War.

While Ronald Reagan quietly issued top secret orders that decimated the Soviet Union, only now being declassified and revealed to the public, his liberal adversaries were telling America how the Soviet Union was the embodiment of an economic miracle, an unparalleled example of effective use of human skills and resources. In the midst of this false assessment of Soviet strength by the liberal cabal and the media, Ronald Reagan and his national security advisors could see the Soviet Union's house of cards shaking and trembling. And while Reagan preached the doctrine of both victory over communism and its ultimate destiny to "...lie on the ash heap of history," his adversaries, and particularly the self-appointed oracles of the media, were heaping immense criticism upon Reagan for his "...myopic belief that America could bring about the fall of the Soviet Union."

I am indebted to the work of Peter Schweizer and to the friendship of Judge William (Bill) Clark for much of the documentation regarding Ronald Reagan's vision and victory with regard to the end of the Cold War. Peter Schweizer's book, *Victory*, (Atlantic Monthly Press; 1994) is the most comprehensive study of the policies and actions of the Reagan administration in taking advantage of perceived Soviet weaknesses to bring about the end of the Soviet Union. Schweizer also edited the papers presented at a symposium held in Washington, D.C. on Monday, February 22, 1999, covering the fall of the Berlin Wall. The printed summary of those papers, entitled *The Fall of the Berlin Wall* (Hoover Institution Press, Stanford University) provided additional details of the Reagan administration's strategic vision that were not available to Schweizer in his research for his book, *Victory*. Schweizer's work provides a masterful and irrefutable documentation of how right Ronald Reagan was and how wrong his liberal critics were.

At the time Ronald Reagan became president, Europe's two most prominent leaders, Helmut Schmidt of Germany and Pierre Mauroy of France, were both solidly on record as advocating appeasement and peaceful co-existence with the Soviet Union. Both men publicly condemned Ronald Reagan's public and private assertions that the Soviet Union could and should be defeated. Both were visibly contemptuous of Reagan in several public appearances. Appropriately, neither will be remembered in history for having made any significant contribution to world peace during their time in public office. It is the leadership of Ronald Reagan, whose election they regarded as some type of bizarre American lapse of judgment, to whom history now gives the clear acknowledgment for having seen through the mists of darkness to the fundamental truth regarding the triumph of western democracy over Soviet totalitarianism.

Attitudes among intellectuals and leaders in the United States were hardly any better. Arthur Schlesinger, Jr. declared after a 1982 trip to Moscow that the Soviet system worked quite well. "I found more goods in the shops, more food in the markets, more cars in the street—more of almost everything, except, for some reason, caviar."

Economist John Kenneth Galbraith lauded the Soviet system in 1984 to be in some respects superior to the liberal economies of the West. "The Russian system succeeds because, in contrast to the Western industrial economies, it makes full use of its manpower," he claimed. 'The Soviet economy has made great national progress in recent years."

Professor Lester Thurow at the Massachusetts Institute of Technology (MIT) said in his textbook, *The Economic Problem*, that the Soviet economy was comparable to our economic machine. "Can economic command significantly compress and accelerate the growth process? The remarkable performance of the Soviet Union suggests that it can. In 1920, Russia was but a minor figure in the economic councils of the world. Today it is a country whose economic achievements bear comparison with those of the United States."

Distinguished sovietologist Seweryn Bialer of Columbia University argued in *Foreign Affairs* that the Soviet system was stable because of how well it functioned. "The Soviet Union is not now nor will it be during the next decade in the throes of a true systemic crisis for it boasts enormous unused reserves of political and social stability that suffice to endure the deepest difficulties."

Nobel Laureate Paul Samuelson put it even more strongly in his textbook *Economics* (1981) when he challenged the assumption that communism couldn't work: "It is a vulgar mistake to think that most people in Eastern Europe are miserable."

It was into this intellectual and political malaise that Ronald

Reagan stepped in 1981. However, far from embracing the prevailing opinions, the President and his closest advisers rejected it. The administration boldly and openly challenged the moral basis of communism and the view that accommodation with Moscow was a necessary fact of life. To the astonishment and consternation of leading intellectuals, the President and members of his administration made no bones about the fact that they saw the Soviet Union as the eventual loser in the Cold War.

"The years ahead will be great ones for our country, for the cause of freedom and the spread of civilization," Reagan told students at Notre Dame University in May, 1981, barely four years after President Carter had delivered his conciliatory speech at the same location.

'The West will not contain communism, it will transcend communism," Reagan said. "We will not bother to denounce it, we'll dismiss it as a sad, bizarre chapter in human history whose last pages are even now being written."

In March, 1981 I sat in Bill Clark's office at the State Department and listened to his end of a conversation with some staff at the National Security Council (NSC) at the White House. It was clear that Clark was very unhappy with way a specific issue had been handled, and with the failure of the NSC staff to anticipate a certain problem. Clark's rebuke was severe. There was no chance of misunderstanding that he thought they had failed to protect the President's policy.

I had known Clark since 1967, when we both entered the state capitol at Sacramento as young lieutenants to Governor Ronald Reagan. Bill began 1967 as the Governor's cabinet secretary, but before the end of the year he was Ronald Reagan's chief of staff. Quiet, soft spoken, unassuming, and ever a gentleman, more than one person made the mistake of thinking these personal qualities indicated a weak and uncertain nature. Nothing could be farther from the truth. Beneath that gracious and accommodating exterior was a character and a will to match any challenge. In a test of strength Bill Clark was like a granite mountain.

From our frequent meetings, I observed the bonding of kindred spirits that came about between Bill and the Governor. There was an evident fusion of character and personality between Ronald Reagan and Bill Clark. The Governor acknowledged and respected Bill's intellectual capacity and moral virtue. When Reagan became President there was no hesitation in asking Clark to be with him in Washington as one of the inner circle. Thus, in January of 1981, Bill became the number two man at the state department, the deputy secretary of state.

In that position Clark gained the experience that prepared him to succeed Richard Allen as the President's national security advisor. With Bill Clark by his side the President had an individual of proven loyalty, competence, and most of all one who shared his vision of the future. I think the synergism of wills between the president and Clark had as much to do with the ultimate victory over communism as any other factor in the Reagan administration.

Edmund Morris, the official biographer of Ronald Reagan, said the following about Bill Clark:

"Judge Clark is the most important and influential person in the first (Reagan) administration, and in fact the only person in the entire two terms who had any kind of spiritual intimacy with the President."

As president-elect, one of the most critical decisions awaiting Ronald Reagan was selecting the individual who would function as a director of the Central Intelligence Agency (CIA). At the time of his election in 1980 Reagan probably had no idea how decimated and weakened the CIA had become. A decade of disastrous events, beginning with the revelation by Senator Frank Church and other liberals within the senate of the identities of a number of foreign operatives in the CIA, followed by the dismissal of some seven hundred key analysts who had been tracking communist activities throughout the world, left the CIA dispirited and devoid of the leadership and the capacity to fulfill its mission.

Whether Ronald Reagan fully understood the gravity of the situation at the CIA in 1980 or not, his decision on who to select as the new director could not have been more inspired. William J. "Bill" Casey, as a young naval officer in World War II, had directed some of the most innovative and effective counter-intelligence activities of the entire war. He had also served as the campaign manager for Reagan during portions of the presidential election of 1980. During the campaign Casey had shared with Reagan some of his experiences with covert operations that had materially weakened the Nazi war effort. The two men had also found that they were in complete harmony of will and vision regarding how the ineffective tactics of the West during the Cold War had to be dramatically altered if victory was to come. Thus, it was an easy decision for Reagan to select Casey to head the CIA. Though many others would participate in events concerning the Cold War, the trio of Reagan, Clark, and Casey were the ones whose combined talents, experience, and moral certitude brought to pass the ultimate victory.

On Monday, February 22, 1999, a symposium was convened at the Willard Inter-Continental Hotel in Washington to examine in detail the policies and people assembled by President Reagan that materially contributed to the end of the Cold War.

Before an audience of over 300 former Reagan administration officials and other policy practitioners—including former cabinet officers and senior military officers, scholars, industry leaders, and members of the press—several of the key architects of Reagan foreign policy offered insights into the roots of a strategy that worked to undermine Soviet power.

This was the first occasion since leaving the White House that

Clark had been willing to speak publicly on his perception of the events taking place which hastened the end of the Soviet Union and the Cold War. In his introduction, Clark noted that he should cut his remarks back because others who had spoken before him had covered much of the same subject matter. Then he went on to provide the insights that only he, with his unique personal relationship with the President, could have seen and understood.

"Nineteen eighty-one gave President Reagan and his team the opportunity to get his domestic house in order, after facing double-digit inflation, soaring interest rates, and record unemployment upon entering office," Clark said.

"At the end of 1981 he called us into the Oval Office and said, 'Our concentration has been on domestic matters this year, and I want to roll the sleeves up now and get to foreign policy, defense, and intelligence, beginning the first week of January' (1982). And he added, 'By the way, lean on our experience in Sacramento. Take a leaf from our book out there in our decision-making process, if you would, and let's get moving.'

"The national security process began with his first scheduled morning meeting in 1982, the president's daily brief, the PDB, prepared by Bill Casey and his team through the night, preceded my nine o'clock Oval Office briefing. That customarily got to the President before he came down from the residence, and by then he had penciled in comments for follow-up by Bill and the agency during the day, supplemented by material from State and Defense.

"Furthermore, we started the process of National Security Decision Directives (NSDD's). Let me explain to those of you who may not be familiar with those designations. Again, in January of 1982, under the direction of Tom Reed, we began, at the President's direction, the study of the overall Soviet threat and what our existing bilateral relations were and what they should be in formulating our Soviet policy.

"The earlier study directive became a continuum, a process up through the first two years, in which our crafted studies would be led primarily by the State Department, recognizing the sensitivities of prior White House NSC's taking the lead away from CIA, Defense and State.

"These study directives developed into decision directives, from number 2 up to120, and these studies and resulting decision directives were important from the standpoint of creating the national security policy for President Reagan and his administration.

"As others have said, Ronald Reagan arrived in Washington with a clear vision, with a clear philosophy that had been developed over many years, and the question arose, 'How do we convert that vision, that foresight into policy, policy into strategy, strategy into tactics?' And thus we come to NSDD—75, in December of 1982.

"I would like to describe part of the covering memo, again borrowing a page from the Sacramento days, the President liked short foundational memos—four paragraphs if possible: the issue, facts, discussion, with the alternatives, and finally the recommendations of the National Security Council members.

"The covering letter to the President in December followed a year's study by every agency involved: State, Defense, CIA, Treasury, the Attorney General, Commerce, OMB, the U.N. Ambassador's office, the Joint Chiefs, United States Information Agency, Energy, U.S. Trade Representative, and the Arms Control Disarmament Agency—all participated and signed off.

"My covering memo stated that U.S. policy toward the Soviet Union would consist of three elements: first, external resistance to Soviet imperialism; second, internal pressure on the USSR to weaken the sources of Soviet imperialism; and third, negotiations to eliminate, on the basis of strict reciprocity, outstanding disagreements.

"We emphasized the second of these objectives, internal pressure on the USSR representing a new objective of U.S. policy.

"It has always been the objective of U.S. policy toward the Soviet Union to combine containment with negotiations, but the attached document to the covering memo was the first in which the United States Government added a third objective to its relations with the Soviet Union; namely, encouraging anti-totalitarian changes within the USSR and refraining from assisting the Soviet regime to consolidate further its hold on the country and its satellites.

"The basic premise behind this new approach was that it made little sense to seek to stop Soviet imperialism externally while helping to strengthen the regime internally. This objective was to be attained by a combination of economic and ideological instrumentalities.

"Thus it became United States policy to avoid subsidizing the Soviet economy or unduly easing the burden of Soviet resource allocations, so as not to dilute pressures for structural change within the Soviet system.

"In the ideological competition, the United States would strongly affirm the superiority of Western values, expose the double standards employed by the Soviet Union in dealing with difficulties within it own domain and the outside world, and prevent the Soviet Union from seizing the semantic high ground in the battle of ideas. The United States should in addition seek to weaken Moscow's hold in its empire, particularly Poland, its hub.

"This was difficult language for some in the bureaucracy. Agriculture, Commerce, State—all had difficulty with the new internal pressures approach as being too aggressive.

"First of all, there was disparity among our intelligence agencies as to how weak the Soviets were internally. Some felt the Soviet economy was quite strong, but President Reagan decided we would take the chance on assisting their destabilization and dissolution.

"Richard Pipes and John Lenczowski, of the NSC staff, warned us in the first days of the administration that never had the Soviets been a greater threat for the simple reason that the Kremlin had reached the conclusion that they had military superiority, both nuclear and conventional, to start and win the war against us.

"Dr. Pipes went on to add, and some staff in the White House attempted to silence him, that war was inevitable unless we were able to change the Soviet System.

"Frankly, there were enough of us who believed that to be the case, and thus, we worked hard on that new policy element of trying to turn the Soviet Union inside itself. And of course, that did ultimately occur.

"Dr. Pipes also noticed, following our several addresses announcing this new approach, that the Soviets were frightened by the new addition. They did not refer to it publicly. They continued calling us adventurous warmongers, but did not acknowledge the new element that we had placed in our policy of attempting to go to their inside in changing the hearts and minds, not necessarily of the Soviet leadership, but more importantly, of their people.

"The NSDD process continued beyond number 75 and included setting up the three Liberty radio stations, the Office of Public Diplomacy, and working on other aspects of public diplomacy, such as the successful *Project Democracy*.

"Another process the President asked us to use, again taking a page from our Sacramento days, was to reach out to others on a bipartisan basis to obtain the support needed from the congress and from the people for his policy of peace through strength. We developed such things as the Kissinger Commission, in which Jeanne Kirkpatrick was heavily involved, to look at Central America—not only at security issues, but also the longer-term social issues.

"We created the Commission on Strategic Forces, which included Brent Scowcroft, Nick Brady, Al Haig, Richard Helms, and others, who were effective in meeting the nuclear freeze movement that was not only attacking our efforts in arms control but also opposing our defense budget.

"These two and other commissions were both bipartisan and effective. At times, we were criticized for reaching outside to the significant people from prior administrations and from the other party, but the approach was effective.

"Other changes that President Reagan brought into being, in contrast to prior administrations, included a standing scheduled meeting with the Joint Chiefs of Staff and their great leader, Jack Vesey. General Vesey, arriving in 1982, was particularly instrumental in the INF effort and modernization of our NATO and nuclear forces in Europe.

"Let me go on to this revisionism effort that seems to be of such concern to our speakers today, that asks whether the Reagan administration is receiving its due credit for bringing down the Berlin Wall.

"If we can repeat the President's favorite admonition, his Cabinet in 1981 at Christmas received an etched piece of crystal, which said, 'You can accomplish anything if you don't worry about who gets the credit.' If he were here to comment on what is going on in academia today, he would tell us, again, not to worry about it. And he would also add another favorite saying of his, 'The truth always rises to the surface. We can hear that in every language.'

"Thus, I think we should take that leaf and recognize that in his courage and selflessness, he never wanted to take credit for his accomplishments. I once heard someone say, 'Congratulations, Mr. President, on your success in ending the Cold War.' He smiled and said, 'No, not my success but a team effort (led) by Divine Providence.'

"In describing the superpower competition, President Reagan rarely used the term Cold War. He called it a 'conflict.' I truly believe that in the time we were together, in Sacramento, and later in

Washington, all of us realized his love of life—and not just life at the moment, but all human life, a belief that drove his every policy decision.

"He always took occasion in his major addresses to mention the sanctity and dignity of all human life. This was again brought to the attention of more than one person upon his seeing the gruesome SIOP presentations in the Situation Room, in which scenarios were shown for how a nuclear war might be fought. He would watch that screen showing the worst of possibilities of such a war, watch the red marks spread as the bomb drops occurred in the Soviet Union as well as on our own population, to really see America destroyed. All eyes focused on him at times as he bit the lower lip, and the question arose: Would he, if necessity came, be able as Commander in Chief to give that terrible order to respond to nuclear attack?

"When John Vesey became chairman of the Joint Chiefs, he asked me that question, 'Would our Commander in Chief be able to act?'

"Remember, we never said 'no first strike.' When the president was asked by a reporter, 'Would we ever strike the Soviets first?' he answered, 'The President never says never.'

"I responded to Jack Vesey, 'Jack, that is a question that you are going to have to ask the President himself.' I told the President the Chairman of the Joint Chiefs wanted to come in with that question, and the President said, 'Fine, Bill.'

"I remember, I took a chair and General Vesey pulled a chair up to the front of the desk and said, 'Mr. President, can you?' And the President said, 'Absolutely, if it becomes necessary. I have taken the oath of office to protect our people, and the first duty of government is survival of its people.' But he would continue to remind us of the sanctity and dignity of human life and our duty to protect it.

"The *evil empire* speech that we have all heard so much about was not so much about the Soviet Union as it was about Ronald Reagan. It was criticized by so many from the media and academia, but to many of us it was probably his greatest speech because it was so much the real Ronald Reagan.

"He, I think, will be remembered by those of us who worked with him in Sacramento and in Washington as being far wiser than his cabinet and his staff combined. I will never forget Ambassador Dobrynin saying, 'We worry about President Reagan, we don't necessarily like him, but he is the one world leader that is totally predictable, and while he may vary his strategy and tactics, he will never vary his principles.' Of course, that courageous person is the man who led us to the victory we are celebrating today."

IBID, pp. 69 to 76: Presentation by William P. Clark

Revised by William P Clark and quoted with his permission

Perhaps of all things that the Soviet leadership feared about Ronald Reagan's presidency was his commitment to the anti-missile defense system, known officially as the Strategic Defense Initiative (SDI) but nicknamed by the media and others as Star Wars. The significance of Ronald Reagan's commitment to the development of the SDI has been well documented and effectively presented.

Any analysis of the end of the Cold War should consider what happened during the summit meeting between President Reagan and General Secretary Gorbachev at Reykjavik. It was the second summit meeting between the two leaders, and whereas the Geneva summit had been a more genial effort of getting acquainted, Reykjavik was a deadly serious crossroads for both leaders. Out of this summit their respective places in history might well have been determined.

The Soviets made remarkable concessions, the sincerity and validity of which were not seriously doubted. Throughout the negotiating sessions Reagan was certain that Gorbachev had not laid all his cards on the table. Others in the U.S. delegation were euphoric at the idea that the Soviets were prepared to concede so much in the way of arms reductions. All Ronald Reagan had to do in order to return home an international hero was to accept the Soviet proposals, and all the world could breathe a sigh of relief.

Then Gorbachev finally presented his ultimate demand. Reagan must agree to abandon the SDI. The Soviets would essentially give the U.S. everything they had sought in the past, but SDI had to go. Reagan understood the real dilemma that Gorbechev faced. The Soviet economy was so weakened internally, and the pressures of captive states wanting to be free of years of deprivation and want, the result of being required to support the Soviet military effort, were approaching the explosive point. Gorbachev could never mobilize the resources to match the U.S. development of SDI. Gorbachev's final requirement to give the U.S. all that they had sought in arms reductions was that the U.S. abandon the SDI.

The President never hesitated, standing his ground with firmness. His answer was a firm and resolute, "no." The summit was reported by much of the media as a foreign policy disaster for Ronald Reagan. In reality, it was one of the several defining moments of his presidency.

One of those who returned with President Reagan from Reykjavik, and who has asked to remain anonymous, described the mood among the senior diplomatic staff as one of depression and agony, as they continued to talk of what might have been. But there was one individual who was quite at peace with himself, who recognized that ultimately Reykjavik was an incredible triumph for the United States. That individual was the President himself, the hand wringing and deep sighs of all the others were of little consequence.

Peter Schweizer summed it up very well.

"The genius of the Reagan administration's approach is not

simply the innovative and unique policies that were employed but the courage with which they were pursued. They were politically risky and went against the assumptions that had guided U.S.-Soviet policy for decades. The Reagan administration rejected containment for something bolder. Ironically, in this boldness, the administration seemed to be heeding the advice of Karl Marx, who wrote in the December 1853 issue of the *New York Tribune*: 'There is only one way to deal with a power like Russia and that is in the fearless way.'

"How historians will ultimately judge the U.S. role in the demise of the Soviet Union remains to be seen, but those at the center of the drama certainly saw a U.S. hand in these dramatic events. When the Berlin Wall was breached in November 1989 and Germans united in celebration, German Chancellor Helmut Kohl is said to have telephoned the White House to thank the United States. And in 1991, on the day he resigned his office and officially declared the USSR dead, Mikhail Gorbachev took the time to write a long personal letter to Ronald Reagan."

IBID, p. 47: *The Fall of The Berlin Wall*

As more classified documents from the Reagan Administration come into the public domain, and as objective scholars take the time to study the documents available at the Reagan Presidential Library, the reality of Ronald Reagan's leadership in ending the Cold War gains greater and greater confirmation. On March 5, 2000, Mr. Frank Warner, of the Allentown Pennsylvania *Morning Call* newspaper, wrote a delightful article that illustrates how often Ronald Reagan *stood alone* in his conviction that the *evil empire* could be defeated. I believe the content of that article will help the reader to understand the sequence of events initiated by President Ronald Reagan that brought the Cold War to its end.

"On March 8, 1983, Ronald Reagan called the Soviet Union the focus of evil in the modern world. *The Evil Empire Speech* disturbed the political universe, but the critical words almost went unsaid.

"President Reagan's *Evil Empire Speech*, often credited with hastening the end of Soviet totalitarianism, almost didn't happen.

"According to presidential papers obtained by *The Morning Call*, Reagan was thwarted on at least one earlier occasion from using the same blunt, anti-communist phrases he spoke from the bully pulpit 17 years ago this week.

"And former Reagan aides now say it was their furtive effort in the winter of 1983 that slipped the boldest of words past a timid bureaucracy.

"With clever calculation, the *Evil Empire Speech* eluded U.S. censors to score a direct hit on the Soviet Union.

"'It was the stealth speech,' said one Reagan aide.

"In the spring of 1982, the president felt the reins on his rhetoric. The first draft of his address to the British Parliament labeled *The Soviet Union the world's focus of evil*. He liked the text. But Parliament never heard those words.

"U.S. diplomats and cautious Reagan advisers sanitized the speech, removing its harshest terms, according to documents from the Ronald Reagan Presidential Library in Simi Valley, California.

"But nine months later, Reagan spoke in Orlando, Fla., and delivered many of the passages deleted from the London address. His Orlando speech is known as the *Evil Empire Speech*.

"The speech alarmed moderates in the West, delighted millions living under Soviet oppression and set off a global chain reaction that many believe led inexorably to the fall of the Berlin Wall and to freedom for most of Eastern Europe.

"The Reagan Library papers provide fascinating insights into the drafting of what may have been the most important presidential statement of the Cold War. They also reveal that, despite the unremitting influences on him, the president himself decided what he would say.

"Arms talks continued, and on December 8, Reagan and Gorbachev met in Washington to sign a treaty eliminating all inter-mediate—and shorter-range nuclear missiles in Europe. It was the first treaty ever to reduce nuclear arsenals.

"Reagan left office in January 1989, after President George Bush's election. Throughout the year, the Iron Curtain showed its torn and rusty fray. Residents of communist East Germany began sneaking west through neighboring nations.

"On November 9, 1989, as the East German government relieved travel restrictions, East and West Germans climbed up on the Berlin Wall. They danced up top (sic), and then they pounded the wall with hammers. Sensing no support from Moscow, East German border guards did nothing to stop them. The Berlin Wall had fallen open.

"1991 was the final year of the Soviet Empire. On June 12, Boris Yeltsin was chosen president in the first free elections ever in Russia. On December 25, after a tumultuous summer and autumn, Gorbachev resigned as leader of the Soviet Union. The next day, the Soviet Union officially came to an end."

On August 17, 1992, at the Republican National Convention, Reagan had his last word on the long struggle. It was a month after the Democratic convention nominated Arkansas Governor Bill Clinton for President.

"We stood tall and proclaimed that communism was destined for the ash heap of history," Reagan told his fellow Republicans. "We never heard so much ridicule from our liberal friends. The only thing that got them more upset was two simple words: *Evil Empire*. But we knew what the liberal Democrat leaders just couldn't figure out: The sky would not fall if America restored her strength and resolve. The sky would not fall if an American president spoke the truth. The only thing that would fall was the Berlin Wall. I heard those speakers at that other convention saying, 'We won the Cold War'—and I couldn't help wondering, just who exactly do they mean by 'we'?"

I began this book with the premise that Ronald Reagan possessed certain qualities of character and fundamental virtues that explained his remarkable success as a political leader. Over the years since we left Sacramento I have used many of the experiences cited in this text in an attempt to teach my children and grandchildren the value of virtue and character. I have used the example of a man who had literally changed the world. It is my prayerful desire that others may find in these pages a greater understanding of this remarkable man, Ronald Reagan, and through his example find a greater understanding of those qualities which can enable someone to rise from whatever their station to a level of personal greatness.

I think it would please Ronald Reagan to know that a book about him was dedicated to the memory of an obscure American boy who died in the jungles of Vietnam fighting in defense of those political principles which Ronald Reagan so intensely believed. U.S. Army Sp. 5 Ross M. Bee died in Vietnam on January 19, 1967, during the first month of Ronald Reagan's tenure as governor of California.

Reagan would often say, in private and in public, "You and I have a rendezvous with destiny." Then he would ask the question, "Will we pledge our lives and our sacred honor?" Before he would reach his twenty-first birthday, Sp. 5 Ross Bee's rendezvous with destiny was indeed, to pledge and to give his life. Ronald Reagan's rendezvous with destiny was to pledge his sacred honor.

Ronald Reagan would be the first to affirm that he believes that somewhere in the American republic there is another obscure boy in whom the hand of deity is instilling the same principles and virtues that were his core character. He would also tell us that when the time of crisis comes, that boy will appear on the American scene, just as Ronald Reagan did, prepared with a vision and able to provide the leadership and courage to see that vision become a reality. We can only pray that when our nation's next great rendezvous with destiny comes, that obscure American boy will be ready and able to follow in the footsteps of predecessors like Washington, Lincoln, and Ronald Reagan.

The author presents to Governor Reagan a copy of his book entitled, *We Dare Not Fail*. The book was inspired by the governor's challenge to the author "...to find a better way." After its publication Reagan endorsed the book as "must reading for my cabinet."

The author discusses with Governor Reagan Proposition 18 on the 1972 California ballot. Reagan endorsed the anti-pornography initiative and genuinely supported its provisions. With the author and Governor Reagan is California State Senator Fred Marler.

Governor Reagan presents jelly beans to the author's son and Native American foster daughter.

Governor Reagan signs his executive order designating the
author as the Chairman of the California State Commission on
Indian Affairs. Watching the governor are the author's son, David,
and the author's Native American foster daughter, Esther.

Ronald Reagan addresses a crowd of 5,000 protestors
at the California Capitol.

Edwin Meese III, with Governor Ronald Reagan. Meese was the Governor's Chief of Staff during much of his tenure as Governor of California, and later became Attorney General of the United States under President Reagan.

The author and Governor Reagan at a press conference.

President Reagan and National Security Advisor, Judge William "Bill" Clark, walking through the portico at the White House. Much of the information contained in Chapter Eleven was provided by Judge Clark.

About the Author

John Harmer resides in Bountiful, Utah, with his wife Carolyn. A native of Utah, John received his law degree from George Washington University in Washington, D.C. For more than twenty years John and Carolyn lived in California, where all ten of their children were born.

John first met Ronald Reagan in the fall of 1962. On several occasions during the next four years they discussed political philosophy and Reagan's potential candidacy for public office. In 1966 Reagan was the Republican candidate for governor of California, while John was the Republican candidate for the state senate in the twenty-first senatorial district. Both were elected to their respective offices. In 1974 John won the California primary election to become the Republican candidate for Lt. Governor. Shortly thereafter he was appointed by Governor Reagan to fill the unexpired term of Lt. Governor.